A Jay in the Jacaranda Tree

John Manuel

Copyright © 2017 John Manuel

First published in English worldwide by
Lulu Press, www.lulu.com

All rights reserved. Apart from any use permitted under copyright law,
this publication may only be reproduced, stored, or transmitted, in any form,
or by any means, with prior permission in writing of the publishers or of the author.
It may not be otherwise circulated in any form of binding or cover other than that
in which it is published and without a similar condition being imposed
on the subsequent purchaser.

Typeset in 12pt Perpetua

Some of the real people in this book have had their names changed.

Front & back cover design and photography by the author.

1st edition.

ISBN 978-0-244-60549-0

Also by John Manuel

The "Ramblings from Rhodes" series
of lighthearted Grecian travel memoirs:
Feta Compli!
Moussaka To My Ears
Tzatziki For You To Say
A Plethora Of Posts

The Novels:
The View From Kleoboulos
A Brief Moment of Sunshine
Eve of Deconstruction
Sometimes You Just Can't Tell

All of the above available from **Amazon** worldwide
in paperback or Kindle format
and from the publisher, **www.lulu.com**

More information about the above titles can be found
on John Manuel's blog:
http://ramblingsfromrhodes.blogspot.com
and on his website:
http://johnphilipmanuel.wix.com/works

*"I disapprove of what you say,
but I will defend to the death your right to say it."*

- Evelyn Beatrice Hall
(under the pseudonym S. G. Tallentyre),
reputedly quoting Voltaire.

A JAY IN THE JACARANDA TREE

The Intro

If you were reckless enough to read my "Ramblings From Rhodes" series (a trilogy …in four parts!), and let's be truthful here, a touch of recklessness now and again does no one any harm, then you'll probably recognise a little of the content in this book. It's inevitable I suppose, given the fact that they contain a lot of stuff about our first few years of living on Rhodes and this one is a reflection of our first decade here.

So, there may be some subjects and events described in this book that ring a bell or two, but hopefully you'll find that I'm coming at it from another perspective, perhaps interjecting a few different details, that sort of thing.

By and large though, I think, nay hope, that you'll find the majority of this book's content to be new and entertaining, educational, philosophical, cerebral… OK, so maybe I should stop there.

If you love Greece, or even if you don't, but you like to read factual books about other places in this big wide world, then I sincerely hope when you put this one down at the end (or turn off your device) you'll perhaps think …time I had a nice stiff drink?

By the way, throughout this book I refer occasionally to the village of Arhangelos. It's more often spelt in English '*Archangelos*', with the '*ch*' as in '*arch*'; but I leave out the '*c*' deliberately, because it means an English-speaking reader will be better placed to pronounce it as do the Greeks, who never call it '*Arch*-angelos'. It's my book and I'll do as I like! Toys out of the pram before we even start then…

1. Bridget Bardot's Hair?

There's a Jay in the jacaranda tree. Nothing too unusual in that for many people perhaps, but for us though? It marks a milestone. We saw that tree planted, when now? Oooh, must have been late 2006, maybe early 2007. Around it at that time was nothing but churned up dust after the builders had finally cleared away a mountain of rubble, old broken blocks and bags of cement, trashed terra cotta roofing tiles and various substances used in building the villa which had stained the lumpy, rock-hard ground in a spectrum of various colours, ranging from white to a mucky, mirky slate grey. There was old electrical cable and plastic trunking, spent paint cans and yellow plastic buckets of "Sto", the substance that was kind of sprayed on to the walls to resemble rendered plaster. There were wooden pallets on which had arrived various materials for the construction of the property and an assortment of discarded screws, nails and wire. There was at least one fairly hefty wooden cable drum, which I eventually salvaged to convert into a garden table, with visions in my head at the time of the two of us, or maybe the four of us (my wife and I, plus our close friends and the owners of the property John and Wendy), seated around it on a warm blue, balmy Greek summer's evening with drinks and nibbles laid out before us while we chewed the fat and admired the view down the kilometre of valley below us and out to the vast blue expanse of Mediterranean Sea.

Along with that fledgling jacaranda were also planted a few young slips of fruit trees, their trunks barely thicker at the time than a man's index finger, their fragile foliage clinging on in the strong breeze that blows across the mountainside bringing a scorching, drying heat like a hairdryer during the long summer months and a cool wind that will 'cut you in half' during January.

Following the builders finally having cleared the site of what would hopefully some day become an orchard in reality as well as in name only, John had ordered a tipper truck-load of "topsoil" to try and enrich the dusty, yellow flour-like dirt that the ground around the villa comprised of to enable it to support the growth of decorative and fruit-bearing plant life. Now, in the UK the word 'topsoil' brings to mind a rich, black loam that's teeming with bug-life and nutrients all just waiting on their opportunity to nurture some freshly planted fruit trees, not to mention a crop or so of vegetables to grace our nightly table. Minerals and trace elements would be in there waiting to give such plants the ability to confront the hot summer wind and the clammy winter gales and the doughty pluck to present us with something to eat some day.

The 'soil' here is the colour of Bridget Bardot's hair when she was young and sexy. There is no other similarity beyond that though. Wait, yes, I'm sure that Miss Bardot's hair would have been a barren place in which to try and grow something edible. So there are two similarities after all.

One day we heard the unmistakable drone of a tipper truck's diesel engine as it laboured up the last steep fifty metres or so of dirt lane to our front gates (only installed a matter of weeks previously) and our anticipation of the task of shovelling, wheelbarrowing and raking the rich, fertile topsoil into the plot became palpable. Here, you can 'dig' over the 'soil' that you inherit if you have a pickaxe on hand to start the process. Once you've done your Cool Hand Luke impression for a few days and managed to break it up to a depth of around a foot, you can then set about trying to fork it over so that, when you water or perhaps even get rain, the life-giving fluid can penetrate below the surface and get to the job of allowing roots to suck up the moisture along with the needed nutrients for healthy plant growth.

The problem is, once it rains (and the rains don't start in any serious way here until at least mid-October in a normal year, having previously fled the scene during the previous May) the dirt turns to a tawny goo that, once it dries out, forms a thick, solid crust that is devoid of any texture and will successfully prevent the water from soaking in the next time it falls on this surface. Thus, you're back to square one, nursing your blisters and massaging your tired biceps and shoulder muscles, you find yourself once again reaching for the pickaxe.

Ah, but we had a solution. A tripper-truck-load of several hundred Euros worth of 'topsoil' was about to come into view. The vast cloud of particle-filled grey-blue fumes drifting up from behind the shrubs along the lane below us testified to the approach of the truck. Once we'd got that load spread over the plot we'd be in business. Oranges would fairly leap off of the young trees the succeeding winter and into our fruit bowl. Lettuces, courgettes, aubergines and onions would probably be 'showable', were the local Greeks to hold annual shows like they do in rural British villages. Here came our soil salvation and we were excited.

The truck rolled up to the gates, whereupon we were quick to swing them open to allow it to enter the compound that one day would hopefully actually look like a garden and not a man-made desert. John set about directing the driver to turn and raise his truck's bed with the hydraulic ram behind the cab and tip the topsoil on to the ground behind it. We were looking forward to getting it spread out and dug in.

You know something? That 'topsoil' looked suspiciously like the same stuff that we already had, it was certainly the same colour. It proved to be the same consistency too. The only difference this stuff was making once the truck driver had taken his money and left was the fact that, in addition to the drab dead dust of the natural surface of the ground, we also had a ten foot high pile of the stuff too, with a circumference that gave the whole pile a decidedly close resemblance to Silbury Hill in Wiltshire, only it wasn't green. It was the colour of Bridget Bardot's hair, back when she'd have been young and …well, you get the picture.

So, here we are, in the spring of 2016 and that jacaranda tree, against all odds, has survived, grown - although it has to be admitted not by much – and to our complete and utter delight, produced a wonderful array of striking blue, bell-shaped flowers for the very first time.

And this morning, since it's mousmoulia [Eng: Loquat] season too, there's a Jay sitting in it, because the Jays absolutely love to steal the loquat fruit and that tree is only twenty metres away.

2. Feelings

Moving around 2000 miles away from all you have known and loved is a bit of a challenge. OK, so a lot of what's going to happen you can calculate. You can, for instance, work out how long it's going to take you to make the journey in a fifteen-year old van with all that's left of your possessions stacked up in the back behind you. You can organise where to stay on the way and you can easily work out what the journey is going to cost you. Once you arrive at your new home you can be ready for a round of visits to various government offices and Police Stations whilst getting your legalities sorted out. You need a tax number, an AMKA number (which only came into affect after we'd been here a few years) and an accountant. That's something else that we'd not realised until we'd been here seven years and thus had to pay a fine for each year that we hadn't completed a tax return.

You can fairly easily work out what furniture you're going to have to buy and perhaps how much you'll spend on a vehicle. You can soon ask around and find out how electricity prices, phone and water bills compare with what you were paying back in the UK.

Lots of other things you can predict, anticipate and project. What you can't legislate for is how you're going to feel.

Travelling across Europe in the van, we had, on several occasions, a mutual feeling of exhilaration as we glanced at each other whilst charging along a motorway in France, Switzerland or Italy, and both knew what the other was thinking. Life isn't about what you possess. It's not about how new or how large your car or house is. It's not about "being somebody". It's really about what gives true satisfaction. I recently watched an interview with George Harrison on YouTube. It was deeply insightful and revealed just how down to earth he'd remained. Despite all the adulation of Beatlemania in the 60's, despite the fact that each time he met someone for the first time they'd fawn over him as if he were some kind of god, he said, in essence, that there is only one thing of any importance in life, something that far transcends retail therapy, the desire for 'things' that so permeates the more affluent countries of the world. The only thing that matters is if you've found the meaning. We're either alive or we're dead, that's why the search for truth ought to transcend everything else. It's largely why the Western world is predominantly unhappy. People have replaced spirituality with materialism and it's a poor substitute.

Nowadays, and nowhere do you find this better illustrated than in an artificial ex-pat community in a foreign country, it's considered by most to be a weakness for someone to be interested in the deeper things. Most are only interested in (at least their public face gives this impression) firstly, the next beer, followed by the next barbecue, darts league fixture, quiz night or neighbour's misfortune, or perhaps spouse. Frankly, I don't believe there is anyone who doesn't break into a sweat now and then while lying awake at three o'clock in the morning and contemplating the futility of it all. So many people really do have a thirst but owing to peer pressure won't admit to it. They simply have to carry on with this façade of being content with the shallow surface things. Can't show a weakness, wouldn't sit well with the pride. Pass me a *Mythos*. Chilled.

I tell you, I can be philosophical with the best of them.

As we trundled down a long gentle incline of several miles toward the Swiss border on our trip over here in August of 2005, we both agreed that to be free of a mortgage, to be free of a regimented existence which was tantamount to being slaves of the material system, and thus of the commercial world that wants to keep us ever searching for that next material 'high', was truly liberating. We could go anywhere, our assets (such as they were) were almost entirely liquid and it felt like we were truly free of those weights that seemed to be ever bearing down on our shoulders in our previous life.

All we needed at that precise moment was a pee. Desperately.

And the traffic queue down to the border control was humungous. At times like these, when you genuinely feel like your tummy's going to burst under the pressure, you start thinking about unorthodox ways of getting some relief.

My mind wandered back to my teenage years when I'd taken part in a family exchange through my school. About twenty or so of us fifth formers were travelling by coach from Bordeaux to Pau, where we were to meet our host families and opposite numbers from the French lycée, having just flown into Bordeaux airport by plane from Bristol. It was the middle of the night and we still had a long way to go before we arrived at the French lycée in Pau to be billeted. One of my chums, Steve Jones, was so desperate for the loo that he began peeing in stages into a metal Band Aid tin which had been hastily emptied of its usual contents to enable him to do so. He was perched down in the emergency door stairwell just a couple of rows of seats forward from the back of the coach. Mr. Gallaway, the Teacher who was accompanying us, was dozing happily next to the bleary-eyed driver and it was largely quiet on board as we ploughed down one long tree-lined avenue after another. This was the 60's, there weren't many autoroutes back then.

In those days you could easily open the top section of the window of a coach, in this case the tops of the windows had a sprung catch that you just flexed and then slid the window along. I was one of the kids sitting along the back row of the bus, so we only had to swivel to see out of the rear window. There was a Renault following us, probably a little too close for comfort. The driver was soon to find out why. It may have been pitch dark, but that car was well close enough for us to make out its marque and see the driver's eyes, reflecting red from the coach's rear lights, especially as we approached the occasional junction.

Steve would stop the "flow" as the Band Aid tin became full, he'd then slide the side window along a couple of inches and empty out the tin, after which he'd commence re-filling it until the task was done. He probably emptied that tin a dozen times. Those tins weren't very big and the pressing need which had compelled Steve to resort to this method of relieving himself was pressing indeed. In fact, I'd go as far as to say it was probably very pressing.

We all of us (that's "all" in the sense of the five of us that were sitting in the back row) swivelled around each time Steve let the tin discharge its contents, in order to see where it went. Of course some of it splashed the rear corner of the bus itself, but sufficient quantities managed to escape that fate and end up splashing the front windscreen of the Renault that was tucked up behind us.

In a way that only schoolboys can, we managed to whoop and holler quietly enough so as not to arouse the suspicion of Mr. Gallaway, the master down at the front, as we observed our pursuer operating his screen washer for the umpteenth time.

He must have been well bemused. It wasn't raining.

So anyway, here we were, my better half and I, bouncing in our seats in the trusty old Mitsubishi van that we'd purchased and prepared for the trip, wondering how much longer we could hold out. The border control booths were in now view, yet it could well be another half an hour before we got through at the rate the queue was moving. Why, oh why, did we have to choose that particular day and time to cross into Switzerland from France when it appeared that the entire country of France was evacuating to gnome-land along with us?

We looked left and right, hoping that it may be possible to stop on the hard shoulder, which would also have meant forfeiting our place in the queue, but when needs must…

There were no trees or bushes, just steep, uncluttered, grassy banks.

A couple of decades earlier, when I'd been sales repping and had plied my way along the M4 from the West Country to London and back again several times a week, I'd had my regular comfort break stops along the hard shoulder. There were certain places where if you stopped, legged it up a short bank and over a wooden fence, you could experience sublime relief in a piece of woodland with your car still in view and the thunderous sound of the motorway traffic still loud in your ears. How a police car never stopped to investigate me for stopping illegally on the hard shoulder I'll never know. I did it that often!

Here we were, though, creeping snail-like down the gentle incline towards the border between France and Switzerland with the tantalising prospect of cafés, motorway service centres or whatever just the other side of that booth, all of which would no doubt have toilets, yet we were in such pain from the pressure.

I'd say our need was pressing. Very pressing.

More than once I threatened the better half against even contemplating letting it go on the van's seat. You know, women have a different waterworks system from us chaps and they can't as easily tie a knot in it as can we, now, can they. How we made it through that border control without serious internal injury I'll never know. The uniformed bloke who inspected out passports and checked out our pre-paid window sticker (the one you purchase in advance that lets you use the Swiss motorway system) before raising the barrier must have thought we were a strange pair indeed. Gazing incredulously at two faces, contorted, purple and exhibiting a couple of manic smiles that left him unsure whether we'd maybe just escaped from somewhere or were about to lob a grenade into his cubby hole surely must have put him off his muesli.

Anyway, four days after setting out at the crack of dawn from a quiet street in Barry, South Glamorgan, Wales, we were driving up the dusty track in Kiotari, Rhodes, to our new home on Tuesday morning, August 23rd 2005, our travelling companions and owners of the property John and Wendy in front of us, towing their jet-rib on its trailer behind their Renault Espace.

We'd all made it. We were here.

And it was flamin' hot.

Of course we lived with the builders for a further eighteen months before we finally had the place to ourselves. Much of that experience is documented, along with a whole bunch of unconnected anecdotes from all over Greece, in the first two *Ramblings* books. This could have had a bearing on how we dealt with the whole experience emotionally though. It certainly had to be a factor. We never quite got used to raising the shutters every morning to find that the small team of three had already been drilling, sawing, grinding and banging since 7.30am. They'd knock off at four in the afternoon, after we'd significantly shortened their actual working hours by supplying them with all too frequent cups of tea and plates of biscuits throughout the day.

Actually, in the more recent years of living out here I've come to fully understand why they did everything slowly …very, very slowly. If you try to walk, leave alone work, at the kind of pace you would in the UK during a Greek summer, you drop from dehydration and sunstroke before you can say *souvlaki*. These days, when I'm gardening, I may find myself thinking when in one section of the considerably large garden that we tend, 'Oh, I need the secateurs'. So, I drop what I'm doing and amble slowly …very, very slowly, to where the secateurs are situated, then return at the same pace. Even doing that creates the need to whip out an already damp hanky to wipe the sweat from my eyes before commencing the pruning.

The reason, though, that I mentioned the builders being constantly around us is to illustrate that we not only had to deal with the feelings that arise from having left our family and close friends to start a new life somewhere very far away, but also with the fact that we were to have no privacy for a very long time too. My wife would only open the shutters after making sure she'd put something on, since it was very likely that one of the workers would be right outside the window, quietly contemplating a trek to a different area in the search for a power tool or something.

Several people told us about the wall too in our first few months here.

"You'll hit the wall. Everyone does." We'd been told. The person I remember most talking about this wall was Roger, one of the three-man building team. The prevailing opinion seemed to be that by far the majority of people who make this move soon come up against an emotional wall which is thrown up by the whole mixed gamut of having made the move, left friends and family, encountered a new culture, encountered aspects of life in that new culture that no amount of forward planning could have prepared you for and so forth. Like I said earlier in this chapter, lots of stuff you can pre-plan when you move abroad but, what you can't legislate for is how you're going to feel once you've been here a while.

Some things you never get used to. You hopefully learn to live with them and if you succeed at that then you'll probably get over, or rather through 'the wall'. When we first arrived we had every intention of spending each July and August back in the UK. To quote Gary, the British bloke who built the house here, when I asked him about the climate on Rhodes, interested to know what the winters were like.

"You only get two shitty months – July and August."

After over a decade of living here I often quote his words to others who pose similar questions to me. When I'm doing an excursion with holidaymakers during the summer season, it's one of the most popular questions they fire at me. "What's it like in winter?" The winter here, as I often explain, can be compared to a good British summer. When I say "some things you never get used to" I also include the Greeks. One could be forgiven for thinking that because they're born here they take the summer temperatures in their stride. They don't. Yes, acclimatisation does occur to a degree, but just about every Greek I know complains in much the same way as we weedy folk from a temperate climate zone when it's 40°C and the humidity is above 70%. I feel really bad when I say to my excursion guests that we really don't like July and August. After all, they come here precisely to experience wall-to-wall sunshine and to be able to suffer in the heat so that they can go home and feel dosed up in readiness for another British winter, or even the rest of a British summer.

Here, we rise in the morning at this time of the year (I'm writing this chapter in July) and sigh with resignation at the lack of cloud cover. My wife says almost every day of our lives that she wishes oh so much that we could have some fluffy white clouds to give some relief from the relentless, merciless sun; even better that we could have a shower once or twice a week. That's a rain shower of course, not the kind where you slip on a plastic cap and sing opera for five minutes. I have one of those once a week whether I need it or not.

When you first get here it's exciting. You can plan barbecues, you can invite people over a few days in advance and know that the weather isn't going to change. You came here to live the dream and the dream was of clear skies and hot sunshine, ad infinitum. As has been said before, be careful what you wish for.

Then there's the guilt. My parents were both in their seventies when we decided to make the move. We agonised for ages over whether it would be right to go so far away and leave them, not to be able to see them more than once or twice a year. There's always this conflict which rears its head when you make a whole host of decisions in life, not just about whether you're going to emigrate, that have you trying to strike that balance between living your own lives and considering the feelings and needs of your kith and kin.

I vividly remember the weekend that my parents spent with us in our South Wales home, which must have been in the summer of 2004, when I was working in my office (we'd converted the garage) as I had some stuff to get done over the weekend for a private client of my graphic design business. My mum came out of the house and brought me a cup of tea and a digestive and then stood behind me watching me fiddle with an image in Photoshop for a while. She evidently wanted to talk.

"All right?" I asked, over my shoulder, in the way that you do.

"Yes, 'spose so. I want to say something, son." She always called me 'son' when it was something of a more serious nature that she wanted to talk about. When I'd been really small it was 'John-pon-a-lon-don' but I won't tell you about that.

"You and Yvonne are thinking about moving abroad aren't you."

Now, at this stage we hadn't breathed a word to either of my parents about our ideas. They were, after all, still only ideas at this stage. We were close to making the decision, but hadn't quite made it yet. We'd both decided that we'd only do it anyway if both of my parents (my wife had already lost both of hers) were in full agreement. If either my Mum or Dad said they'd not be able to bear it, or that they felt that we ought to stay to be there for them, we'd have put the whole thing on the back-burner for a few more years. Fortunately, despite my father having had a triple by-pass and a pacemaker fitted some years earlier, they were at this time both in strapping health and very active. They were regular travellers abroad, having been to my aunt's house in Florida twice for months at a time, had holidays in Ireland, Italy and all over the UK, and thus there didn't seem to be any urgent need for us to be there to care for their needs on a permanent basis. Neither had smoked for decades and they were comfortable financially.

"Can't keep anything from you for long, can I?" I replied. My feeble attempt at humour.

"Your father and I have talked about it. We want you to know that whatever you decide to do, you'll have our blessing, son. You mustn't de-rail your lives on account of us. We thought that you may be wondering whether we'd try and stop you from going. So we decided that you ought to know our feelings on the subject. It's your lives, you go on and live them."

"Yebbut," I replied, extremely touched by my parents' foresight and unselfishness, "we'd be a long way away and wouldn't be able to see you quite as often as we do now. If you really think that would be wrong, we'll put the idea off until, well, you know, until you no longer need us."

"Look how it is now though," she countered, "We see you several times a year for long weekends. If you were in Greece – it is Greece you're thinking about isn't it – you'd probably come back to see us, or we could come over there and we'd spend weeks together. Probably end up spending just as much time per year with each other as we do now, only in bigger chunks of time."

It was this conversation that was the turning point in our decision-making process. From that point on, and I re-live the moment frequently, we started making plans in earnest, which is not to say that we still didn't question ourselves from time to time during the months leading up to the departure date.

Once we were over here the feelings of guilt still reared their heads on occasion. I'd have to be frank and say that, right up until we'd eventually lost both of them, which was in the summer of 2013 when my mum died, every time the telephone rang my heart would be in my mouth. Over the years from 2005 up until my dad went, which was January of 2009, we'd shot back to the UK a few times when he'd had an issue that involved his being taken into hospital. Some years previously, in fact it would have been 1978, my dad had his first major heart attack and he had it at the very moment when had I walked into his kitchen, having parked my motorbike in their garden in order for it to stay there for the next two weeks while we were in Greece on holiday. Dad was planning to drive us to the airport. Of course, I said we weren't going. No way could we go off on holiday while dad was in a life-threatening medical situation. Yet my mother, who'd called the emergency services while I helped dad into his favourite armchair, told me in no uncertain terms that there was nothing we could do and that he'd be a lot more distressed while in hospital if he thought that he'd ruined our holiday plans.

I guess I had a pretty good set of parents. Of course I have a sister too. She'd spent many years overseas because her hubby was in the RAF, but a few years before we began to talk about upping sticks, they returned to live permanently in the UK and were well prepared to take up the baton, as it were, of being primary look-outs for our parents' welfare. This ameliorated our guilt feelings to a large degree and so plans were set in motion.

We were going to Greece.

3. Climate

It still bemuses me that ex-pats who've lived here for years complain about the heat during July and August. I mean, duh?

It's probably true that, unless any of us have lived in Greece for those entire two months before moving out here, no one is truly ready for the oppressiveness, the constant, persistent, unabating sweatiness and exhaustion that daily temperatures in the mid-to-upper 30's (that's upper 90's to you American folk) can evoke within one.

At first, of course, it's terribly exciting. We arrived here during the third week of August, having not only left the UK with temperatures in the upper teens or low 20's, but also having driven through a deluge in Switzerland and Italy en route. So, when we awoke, dressed and drove off the ferry in Rhodes harbour on August 23rd 2005, it was dead good to feel hot and sticky. It was exhilarating to see that endless blue sky. Now we were going to experience the real life.

Right from the "off" we began to understand the difficulties that the summer climate can bring. After all, if you don't have any mains electricity then you also don't have air-conditioning. If you can't get the breeze to blow through your room at night then you sleep in a constant pool of sweat. The sheets, the pillow, your body – are all not just damp, but wet. Our water pressure was also pathetic for the first several months, owing to the fact that the supply was a big see-through tank on the bank behind the house, which meant that we had to move around in the shower to get wet; that is the kind of "wet" that one would like to be, as opposed to the kind of sweaty "wet" that one actually was whilst trying to get some sleep.

The novelty of day after day of sunshine and intense heat soon wears off when it goes beyond a couple of weeks, the kind of duration that most people's summer holidays would be. As I mentioned in the previous chapter, you don't ever get used to it, but you do learn to live with it. There is a difference.

I also mentioned in the previous chapter that when we're asked about the winter weather by people on their holidays out here, we often reply that it's like a good British summer and that we prefer the winter months to the summer ones. In winter, there are days when it's exhilarating to be alive, to go outside at dawn and feel the freshness in the air, see the deep blue of both the sky and the sea, and note the crisp, defined line of the horizon, indicating that humidity is low. The colours of the landscape are vivid, almost rich, due to the rains that fall from time to time. Here in winter, on average it rains on about nine or ten days each month. You do occasionally get a grey day, with rain that could perhaps be described as drizzle, but these occasions are rare. More often than not the rain follows a three-day cycle. The clouds begin to accumulate on the first day, perhaps blocking out the sunlight by midday or mid-afternoon. During the first night or the second day the heavens will open with positively deluge-like force, bringing stories from the book of Genesis to mind, there will be fork lightning and thunder will crack above you like you are in a war zone. Maybe once or twice in an entire winter the precipitation will include hailstones, which can be of the variety that are at least marble-sized, sometimes the size of a golf ball, certainly often big enough and falling hard enough to damage cars. The next day, though, the skies will clear. You may even wake up to the big horizon-to-horizon blueness once again. The air will be fresh and smelling wonderful and the plant, insect and animal life will all be rejoicing in the refreshment.

On days like that we just have to get outside. Walking in the hills behind this house, where you can often scan the horizon at points along the lanes and see nothing man-made, is an adventure in biology and botany. There may be deer, often right outside our gate in the murk just before dawn. There are soaring Golden Eagles and other birds of prey. In January the wild flowers begin to put on their annual show in earnest and will continue to delight the eye right through until the dryness of June finally sends the vegetation back to its dusty, pale wind-burned raggedness as the plants dig in for several months of dry, scorching, arid endurance. They will then wait it out for the first rains in dogged determination, which frequently involves simply existing, flowerless, dust-covered, dry.

The wild anemones of a Rhodean winter, though, are a riot of enthusiasm for weather that involves warm sunshine (as opposed to boiling hot), cloud and sunny intervals, rain and showers. We don't get showers all that often, since when it rains it's usually a case of "batten down the hatches" for another storm, but we do get them from time to time. In fact, even here in Rhodes a Greek friend, when I asked him about the weather in April many years ago, replied:

"Oh, you know, April showers." I couldn't believe my ears.

I have since come to understand the truth of his words though. In fact, spring time is the one time of the year when people in the UK seem to have this fixation with comparing their weather with what we're getting down here in the Med. The media love headlines like "Warmer in Gateshead than Greece!" It is true that during the months of March and April the daylight hours are very similar in the UK to what they are here. It is also true that for maybe a week or two the daytime temperatures may be comparable, but not, though, the evening or overnight ones. What does it matter anyway? This is Greece, that is the UK, where is the point in making such comparisons?

Winters here are never dull. Occasionally, during the months of November through February, we'll see twisters out on the bay, maybe a mile or two out from the shore. They're water spouts that sometimes occur more than one at a time. From our vantage point quite high on a hillside one can even watch them form if the weather conditions are right. That would mean leaden grey skies and more often than not rain falling. These twisters are harmless enough when they stay out on the bay. Well, maybe not to the occasional fish or other sea life that may suddenly find itself several hundred feet above the surface of the water after it had been going about its usual sealife kind of business, paying no mind to anybody.

The problem is when they approach the shore.

Just once, possibly in the winter of 2009-10, but I could be wrong, one of these "tornadoes" actually did come ashore, making its landfall at the beach below the village of Gennadi. It was late in the day and the light was failing fast when it completely destroyed one of the three tavernas situated right on the beach there. Taverna Klimis wasn't there any longer when the sun rose the following day. The funnel took a random course through Gennadi, then along the coast toward Kiotari and up the valley to our house, our houses in fact, because fifty metres up the hill from us there are two more detached properties.

Tracking inland from the beach it ripped the head off a cow that was tethered in a field behind the beach and tore the roof off of a one-storey dwelling beside the main road below the village. The poor unfortunate bovine lost its head it seems as a direct result of its being tethered with a strong rope to a post driven into the ground, owing to the fact that the patch of land where it lived had no fences. Under normal circumstances the hapless creature was quite content, since during the winter months that area is usually green and lush. The rope having held fast, the only thing that could give was the cow's throat and thus, well, it did.

There were all kinds of properties that sustained minor damage. We had gone to bed owing to the fact that the electricity had gone off (no surprises there then) and heard a horrendous clacking and banging noise from above while quaking under the duvet. There was nothing that could be done until daylight and so we sat tight and awaited the storm's passing. It passed eventually after another hour or so of frighteningly strong winds and then a dead calm set in. The next morning, as per usual, dawned bright and sunny as though the weather was a recalcitrant child in whose mouth butter wouldn't melt. About a dozen ridge tiles had been ripped rom our terracotta roof, exposing the felt and timber frame beneath. Pieces of smashed tile lay on the path around the house.

It didn't take us long to source a local tradesman who, to his credit, came within 48 hours and made good the roof, even mixing a red colour with the mortar to try and match the existing stuff. The job he did wasn't half bad. Our neighbours up the hill had sustained similar damage, only not to the house, but to their car port, which has the same kind of roof as the house. Dimitri the odd job man was well pleased because, as soon as we'd pressed the cash payment into his palm he had his next job lined up just a few yards up the hillside.

One sound you really don't want to hear during the summer months is a *Canadair*. If you're anything like I was when I first got here you may just not even know what a Canadair is. If you live in a temperate climate where the only sight you ever get of forest or hill-fires is on the TV news reporting on places far away, you'll have no cause to know anyway. My parents often used to talk to me about the war years in the UK when, even as teenagers, they'd learned to distinguish between the sounds of various aircraft engines. Notwithstanding the fact that there were air-raid sirens, they'd nevertheless stop in their tracks, in fact just about everyone everywhere would do so, if the sound of a propeller-engined aircraft reached their ears. Well, there weren't jets then anyway. There were times when the sirens wouldn't wail and yet a lone enemy plane would fly overhead, usually running out of fuel and separated from its squadron. I remember as a boy being shown green craters in the countryside around my home in the West Country and being told:

"That was where a German fighter crash landed. The pilot [if he'd survived] was taken into a local home and given first aid, a meal and a bed for the night, then on the next day given over to the authorities."

My Dad said they knew if a plane was "one of ours" or "one of theirs" by the tone of its engine. Of course, these days most planes are jets, or at the very least prop-jets, but the Canadair drones like an aircraft from the days of the war, since its engines are propeller-driven. They need to be owing to the speeds at which they fly. Jets would be much too fast for the job at hand, which is to fly low over the ocean, scoop up a load of seawater (often with a variety of sea life still in it) then fly over the fires and dump the lot in an attempt to dowse the flames. Canadairs are by necessity piston-engined aircraft and thus sound a lot like a plane from the era of the Second World War. In this part of the island we don't hear many aircraft at all, apart from the occasional fighter jet(s). Civil aircraft flying over our part of Rhodes are usually at full flying altitude and thus only appear to us a glinting silver flashes vapour-trailing across the sky far above.

If we hear the sound of a prop-engine then it's almost certainly a Canadair and that can mean only one thing, there's a fire. Not many summers pass without a few breaking out somewhere on the island. Usually they're quickly contained and with the help of the Canadairs equally as quickly extinguished before they can do too much damage. There have been a few exceptions though.

One such was in 2008, the same year we experienced the big quake. The quake had been an experience in itself anyway. I've been in Greece on several occasions when earthquakes occurred, the most notable if which was one on Kefallonia in the 1980's, which happened while we were taking a siesta and woke us up. There had even been the occasional tremor when I'd lived in South Wales. The 2008 quake on Rhodes was, however, the real deal.

It was July 15th, high summer, when the sun rises impossibly early and the temperatures are invariably uncomfortable for most of the time. At 6.26am the earth in Kiotari shook for twenty seconds. Count them and you'll see that twenty seconds is quite a long time when everything around you is jigging about alarmingly. Many devastating earthquakes last for a considerably shorter duration and cause much more destruction than did this one. Twenty seconds was long enough for the quake to wake us up, allow us to jump out of bed, slip on a robe and walk through two interior doors and outside on to the drive and ten metres from the house before it stopped. OK, so we walked pretty briskly, but that's the way it happened. Plus, of course, we live in a bungalow - so no stairs.

The only damage caused on Rhodes was a small amount of falling masonry and some cracks in buildings, primarily in Rhodes Town. Our home, being constructed of a steel skeleton and thermal-panelling walls, sustained no damage whatsoever. In fact, I remember when our landlords John and Wendy were discussing the building system with us, they told us that the builder had assured them that a house like this could probably withstand a quake of 12 on the Richter Scale with no problem. If the hillside where it's situated were to give way and the house were to slide down the valley, it would still be habitable when it came to a halt, only with a different view. Maybe without water and electricity though, dammit.

This quake was measured at 6.4 on the Richter Scale, big enough to have caused serious loss of life and major damage in urban areas in some countries. In fact, at ten minutes to three the following morning there was also an aftershock of 4.8, par for the course needless to say. There was actually one death from the first quake. This was only due to the fact that a grandmother had panicked, I think in the village of Massari a little north from here, ran outside and tripped, striking her head on a concrete step. We slept right through the aftershock.

According to reliable sources, the main quake was felt as far away as Libya to the south west and Damascus to the east of Rhodes.

Frankly, all told, we could be described as having had a lucky escape.

Then came the fires.

Not more than a week after the quake we began to smell burning outside the house. It didn't take long for blackened pine needles and ash to begin falling from the sky all around the house and garden. To the north and west, over the hill behind us, the smoke began billowing and spreading at an alarming rate. Within three or four days the entire northern half of the sky was the same colour as a cup of strong tea and we were getting seriously worried. Toward the horizon, which to us in that direction is a hill behind the house, you could see the flickering glow of the flames. The Canadairs were soon flying so low over the house that we could eyeball the pilots. One of them had a leaky pair of doors in its underbelly, where it retains the water which it's going to drop on to the fires, and we were sprayed with seawater as it flew across the sky above us.

By the time the fires were into their third day and really getting serious, several other countries had sent their Canadairs to lend a hand with the fire-fighting operation. The Russians even sent a huge great, very strangely-shaped helicopter, which had a spout like an elephant's trunk that it would lower into the sea while hovering a few feet above the surface, in order to suck up the water that it was going to drop on to the flames inland.

We went down to the beach for a swim several times during the time that the fires raged and would tread water while watching the aircraft coming in low over the bay to collect their loads. The Canadairs would fly in procession, sometimes seven or eight at a time, it was really that bad.

Something else that had never occurred to us before moving out here is the fact that the Canadairs can't fly after dark. The altitude at which they work would make it simply too dangerous. As the sun would set day after day, as we wondered whether the house would be safe or not, the sky behind us took on a flickering glow like something out of Dante. The feeling of helplessness that one experiences at such times as the last firefighting aircraft recedes into the distance, heading back to the runway for the night, is very disconcerting. You're at the mercy of the winds, pure and simple.

During the fires we had John and Wendy in next-door for a two week holiday with one of their sons and his young family. Their daughter-in-law even packed her cases and declared that she was ready to go home, she was that worried. She had good reason to be. When the fires were finally put out after over a week of worry we were once again able to take a walk up into the hills behind the house. There is a deep valley not more than one kilometre behind us and the devastation that had been wreaked along it was horrifying to behold. Earthmoving machines had cut swathes through the pine forests to try and create firebreaks, but they hadn't done a lot of good. It was all too little too late. It became very apparent that, had the winds changed direction from westerly to north-westerly while the flames were still raging then our home would be no more. We would have become homeless, of that there was no doubt.

Just a couple of kilometres along the coast from us, towards Glystra, there are beach hotels from which all the guests were evacuated, owing to the fact that they were eastward of us, hence downwind, and the smoke from the fires, which had been moving relentlessly in that direction before they were extinguished, had already enveloped them like a smog.

We had a lucky escape. During the height of the whole episode, I took to going outside at two or three in the morning and staring at the menacing glow over the hill. The air was thick with burning and the constant rain of ash and burnt pine needles frightening. During the daylight hours, while the aircraft droned on without a break, the sky at its worst stage was two thirds dark brown, and this at a time when it ought to be deep blue from horizon to horizon.

Several villages were almost completely surrounded by the fires. Laerma was one of them. Huge numbers of livestock were burned alive. A Greek friend who drives a JCB spent a week after the fires had been put out digging trenches up near that village and burying dead animals, both domestic and wild. They included horses, donkeys, pigs, cattle and deer.

How did this inferno get started? We heard all sorts of rumours. It seems that the most likely cause had been an old farmer up in a remote village thinking that he could get away with having a bonfire of old leaves and stuff in his *"ktima"* (plot of land). Newspaper articles suggested that, once the thing got under way, several young arsonists decided to add to the fun. The result was the worst bush/forest fire for over a decade and, as I write this in December of 2016, the scars left by this fire are still evident over many hectares in the hills of southern Rhodes. Every year there are fires, of course, but more often than not a couple of days and they're dealt with. The Canadairs though will fly over the doused area for at least a day after they've put the fires out, because embers still smouldering can very easily be fanned by the hot summer wind into more flames that can quickly get another fire started if left alone.

The winter rains that occur normally during a Rhodean winter didn't come last year. The winter of 2015-16 was exceptionally dry and led to a serious water crisis on the island this season. As the summer season of 2016 drew to a close water pressure was dropping in some villages, and the supply was being cut off for days at a time in others, to help preserve water stocks. If you read literature about the water supply situation on Rhodes from decades ago, you'll usually find it refers to the fact that this island is well-blessed with fresh-water springs in the hinterland and thus the normal long dry summers don't pose a major problem to the water supply for farmers, businesses or residents. In the last twenty years though things have changed markedly. The rate at which new tourist accommodation is now being constructed seems to bear little relation to the development of infrastructure to meet the demands for water that all this is placing on the system. It genuinely frightens me to see how huge the swimming pools are that new hotels are being built with. There is no longer simply the "hotel pool", there are dozens of individual plunge pools for the more select rooms, there are common pools that run along the front of some blocks of rooms so that guests can take a dip right outside their terrace, perish the thought of having to make the trek of a few metres to the regular pool with the bar and sun beds all around it.

All of this would be fine and dandy were it not for the fact that the water supply is not increasing at anywhere near the rate needed to satisfy the thirst for these huge virtual villages. In fact, the water supply is hardly increasing at all. Perhaps the real solution would be the installation of several desalination plants discretely placed around the island. Even better, the tour operators could start re-directing people to the joys of staying "small" and experiencing the real Greece instead of their steamroller approach toward ever more all-inclusive resorts which are destroying the local business at an alarming rate.

But then, pigs may indeed start to sprout wings and take off into the blue.

Rhodean winters, as I frequently say, do resemble British summers. Rhodes, of course, has quite a different climate from mainland Greece.

Athens, for example, is over four hundred kilometres to the west and north of us. Thessaloniki is more than six hundred and fifty, due north-north west. The climate in the Dodecanese chain of islands is milder than the rest of Greece in winter, although slightly cooler in high summer. This doesn't mean you can rule out the occasional winter cold spell though. Watching the TV weather forecasts, which we do religiously, the chart showing the entire European continent occasionally shows a cold air mass coming down from the Ukraine, across the Black Sea and Asia Minor and kissing these islands with its blue tinge. At such times the temperatures do take a tumble.

As an example, I'm writing this on December 14th 2016, a couple of days after we had a reading of 25°C in the shade outside the house. Today, however, although there isn't a cloud in the sky, it's struggling to reach 14. It's due to one of these air masses. Those Urals have a lot to answer for. Overnight last night the temperature on our Maximum-Minimum thermometer registered a gnat's whisker under 5°C. That's an exception, but it does illustrate the wisdom of having a log-burner.

It also makes us exceedingly thankful for the construction method used in building this house. Our internal walls are plasterboard, *'gypsosanida'* to a Greek or *sheetrock* as I believe the Americans call it. Or is that *drywall?* Maybe Sheetrock is a brand name. Never mind, I'll leave that in. May get a sponsorship deal or something, eh?

The exterior walls are composed of large sheets of double-skin metal with a thermal foam filling. These are then coated in a fibre mesh and a coating applied like rendering on top of that. This synthetic coating is amazingly resilient and doesn't need painting from year to year, as do the rendered walls of most Greek houses. To clean the outside walls simply requires a hose pipe (if you can justify the use of the water nowadays) and a brush. Job done.

There is a good-sized cavity between the outer and inner walls in which the steel frame of the house is positioned. The only drawback we have is that we have to use expanding wall-plugs when we hang anything on an interior wall. Small price to pay when the weather turns chilly, as it is today. Traditionally-built Greek houses are concrete frames stuffed with blocks and then rendered on both sides. No cavity. The upshot of this is that when the weather's really cold the interior walls are always cold to the touch and frequently "sweat" condensation. Almost every concrete-framed house I've ever been in suffers from black mould at least on the upper interior walls and usually on the ceilings. All the Greeks and ex-pats who live in such properties stoically accept the need to use strong cleaning agents to get the mould off the walls in spring, plus to spend a few hundred Euros most years on paint for a new coat on the exterior walls, which begin to peel almost annually. They advertise de-humidifiers on the telly out here during winter.

Then of course you have the flat roof problems. Most roofs have a couple of air-conditioning units mounted on them, probably too a pole for the TV antenna or dish. They frequently have the flue from the *So'ba* (wood-burning stove) thrusting skyward right through the horizontal surface as well. All such fittings can result in water leaking into the house if these things aren't fitted correctly, which is far too often the case.

Our landlords John and Wendy were wise to take advice from the person who built this house and they plumped for a pitched terracotta tiled roof. When it's cold outside, like it is today, our interior walls are pleasantly warm to the touch and we don't get any leaks from above. No condensation either which means no mould spores which means less health hazards.

Like so many Brits who move out here, we had never experienced a Rhodean winter before we found ourselves living here. Without exception, no one really knows what to expect.

My wife often reminds me of the words of her sister, who, while we were still teenagers "going out" many years ago, had lived and worked for a few years in Athens. Had her Greek fiancée not cheated on her (that's another subject, right there, eh?) she may well have never returned to the UK to live. She often used to say to my wife, "I've never been so cold in my entire life," when referring to Athenian winters in an apartment in the city. The thing is, winters in Greece are short. The worst of the cold weather is confined to a couple of months, unlike the UK, for example, where you can start getting frosts in September and not see the last of them until June arrives. This, according to my theory, is why the Greeks just put up with sweating, mouldy walls in bone-chilling houses during winter, because it doesn't last long enough to have gone to the expense of using building methods that take the possibility of freezing weather into account.

Back in the seventies too, when my sister-in-law was in Athens, there was no such thing as central heating in Greece. It's still relatively rare even today, although we do have friends in Thessaloniki whose entire apartment block has recently been fitted with a gas-boiler system that provides winter heat through conventional radiators for every apartment in the building. All the residents paid for the system collectively. Such things are still, though, the exception, not the rule.

Then you have to take into account the floors. A wooden floor is as rare as hen's teeth in Greece. Most consist of ceramic tiles or crushed marble and it's like walking on the ground at the South Pole during a cold winter's night. Even here on Rhodes most of our Greek friends have a mis-matched selection of rugs and throws which they dig out from their apothikis in December and chuck over every spare square metre of floor or on top of cold leather (or more likely PVC-covered) sofas to make the whole 'sitting down in the dark evenings' thing more tolerable.

Some time ago on the blog I went into the subject of hot water bottles. Whilst we do have a few Greek friends who have electric blankets, most do not and prefer to use a hot water bottle. Not the kind that springs to mind if you live in a colder clime though. A Greek hot water bottle is usually an old plastic 1.5 litre drinks bottle which they'll fill with warm water (too hot and the bottle goes out of shape and may even leak, so no boiled water) and sometimes wrap in a towel. They're nothing if not resourceful.

I remember not long after we had begun to experience our first Rhodean winter, which as it happens was an unusually warm and dry one, going out in search of a traditional hot water bottle. Well, two actually. No sense fighting over it.

In the UK just about every supermarket sells hot water bottles. Here, we almost gave up the search when we couldn't find them anywhere. We searched high and we searched low, we visited every likely store on the island, no luck. Then, in desperation, while I was trying to describe in rather inadequate terms what we were trying to get hold of to Petros, one of the first friends we made out here, he said:

"Have you tried a pharmacy?"

Of course, we hadn't. Why would you have to go to a pharmacy for such a run-of-the-mill product as a hot water bottle? No harm in trying though, so we did.

Amazing. I walked into a pharmacy in Arhangelos and, after first having checked the Greek for "hot water bottle" (*thermofo'ra*), I took a look around. Nothing evident. Oh well, I thought, may as well ask.

"Oh, yes, just a minute," the pleasant young lady assistant said, and disappeared through the door behind her, well out of reach of the customers. She could be heard rummaging around and eventually re-emerged with a nice pink British-looking hot water bottle, a triumphant look on her face. In fact it had the words "British Standard" plus a few numbers moulded into the top.

"Um, could we perhaps have two?" I asked, wondering if there was some kind of government limit on how many hot water bottles the public could purchase at one time. It turned out that they only had the one left in stock. Ah well, we'd just have to be content with that for the time being.

Couldn't help thinking though that it seems that here in Greece hot water bottles are considered only marginally less of a hazard to the public's health than Class B drugs. All those dope-smoking druggies with their rubber hot water bottles sitting in squats in Athens, eh?

A phenomenon one soon gets used to here is the *Afrikaniki skoni*, African dust. I seem to recall that on very rare occasions this has even been known to reach the UK, but here it's an annual event. As the days begin to lengthen in March and April and the weather begins to warm up, the weather forecasts soon start showing the progress northward across the Mediterranean Sea of vast clouds of red dust, which originate in the Sahara. Sometimes vast swathes of the stuff are shown covering all of Greece, parts of Italy and Turkey and further North into Bulgaria, for example. On days when it's not going to rain it's rarely a very big problem, it simply makes the sky a little more hazy and often isn't discernible at all on very clear days. The African dust can come on clear days or it can be mixed into vast cloud masses. When it's combined with cloud it can change the colour of the sky markedly.

When we get rains at the same time as the dust arrives, that's when it really irritates. You don't really see it until the rain clears, but as everything dries up you become aware of a pink, sometimes brown, and even occasionally (and slightly weirdly) greenish dusty coating covering every surface. You can go outside in bright, spring sunshine and find your patio umbrella and furniture, the tiles on your terrace, if you're not careful your washing and certainly your vehicle all coated in the stuff. It's horrendous and sometimes, just as you finish cleaning it off of everything, the next wave will arrive. It can keep coming, on and off, for weeks, usually abating once high summer is upon us. You find yourself just hoping that it won't rain as the next swathe sweeps across the sky. Then, and only then, does it not cause too much trouble.

So, there we are. A potted summary of the climate here on Rhodes. The winters only last a couple of months and the summers last forever. It can be bone-chillingly cold, yet a few months later so hot you think that you got into the oven with the turkey. Something we often remark on is the temperature difference between summers and winters. Although it could be an awful lot colder for a lot more time in the UK, invariably the coldest winter temperatures in South Wales where we'd lived before making the move were probably just a little below zero °C. The highest in summer was more often than not even the mid-twenties, with the occasional (very occasional) exception when a heatwave would take it up to maybe thirty. So the differential would be 25°C average difference for a twelve month period. Here on Rhodes it can reach single figures, in fact even below 5°C, if only on and off, for a couple of months, but in summer it's guaranteed to be 40° and a little more during July and August, thus making the differential 35 to 40° between a winter night and a summer's day.

Well, variety is the spice of life, eh?

4. Politics

Now, before anyone writes in, let me preface this chapter by explaining my stance on this subject. Firstly, I'm a rather apolitical animal. You may or may not agree with me, but then, isn't that what freedom of expression's all about?

Example: why is it that some so-called democratic countries actually punish those who don't vote with fines or even prison sentences? That's not democracy in my book, it's totalitarianism. If someone exercises their right (which it should be in a true democracy) not to vote then that is democracy in action.

I have a CD by Steve Earle, the American musician, and on the sleeve notes it says "If you don't vote – don't beef". I think he sums it up rather succinctly there. If someone chooses not to vote then that very course of action is a "vote" for non-involvement. It's a right that is implied by the very notion of democracy. The key is, those who don't vote have no right to beef. I accept that. If you're going to gripe about the government or its policies and decisions, then you have to have voted. Otherwise you have forfeited the right to be involved in any debate. But to make that decision has to be a fundamental right in a free society.

So, in this chapter I'm coming at it as a bemused observer, a political layman if you like, which is probably what most ex-pat Brits who come here are, at least at the outset.

When we arrived in Greece in summer 2005 everything seemed rosy in the garden. Kostas Karamanlis and his New Democracy party were in power and most people had no idea what was brewing behind the scenes. No doubt there were folk in the know, like the bloke who became Finance Minister under the first ever Syriza government which took power in January of 2015, Yanis Varifocals, sorry Varoufakis, but most people had no inkling of what was to come.

See, the first thing I notice that's wrong with the system here is that there are simply too many parties. There are so many that it's an incredibly difficult task for any individual party to win an overall majority in an election. In fact, something that many are unaware of is that Syriza, who are in power under Prime Minister Alexis Tsipras while I write this, is in fact not a party at all, but rather a coalition of at least six parties. Even if you count Syriza as one party (which as you've just seen - it isn't) these are the current political parties existing and campaigning every time there's an election in Greece:

New Democracy

Golden Dawn

Panhellenic Socialist Movement (PASOK)

Communist Party of Greece

The River *(not so far as I am aware, a tribute to the great Bruce Springsteen album)*

Independent Greeks (ANEL)

Union of Centrists (EK)

Popular Unity

Ecologist Greens

Democratic Left

Christian Democratic Party of the Overthrow (XRIKA)

Reformers for Democracy and Development

Course of Freedom

Society First

Popular Unions of Bipartisan Social Groups

Drassi

Popular Orthodox Rally

Movement of Democratic Socialists

More souvlaki for the downtrodden (OK, I made that one up)…

…plus about twenty more (true!).

Get the picture? In the USA there are two parties, the Democrats and the Republicans. In the UK, granted, there are a few more, but by and large it's still a three or four horse race. Even then, the UK has recently seen a coalition government go virtually the full term when the Conservatives and the Liberal Democrats were uneasy bedfellows from 2010 until 2015, the first coalition government in the UK since the Second World War.

Looking at the picture here in Greece one can see from the outset how unstable the system is. Small wonder that election follows election as no party finds it easy to win a clear majority. Of course the same applies here as in virtually every other democratic country on the planet too, which is: once a party wins the general election there's the short honeymoon period when their supporters shout about how the world's now going to be an infinitely better place. A few months then pass and it becomes clear that no miracles are going to be worked and the disillusionment sets in. Before long there are calls for another general election, people want 'change' and off we go again. Animal Farm.

Never has the expression 'talk is cheap' been more true than during election campaigns. Of course Mr. Karamanlis, on realising that something was soon going to hit the fan, especially as his party had presided over the vast expenditure of cash the country didn't have that was the staging of the Olympic Games in Athens in 2004, called an election in 2009 in full awareness that he'd be defeated. That gave him the chance to get out of the kitchen owing to the intense heat that was building day on day. PASOK got in under the new leader George Papandreou and he very soon declared to the country the truth about the state of the Greek finances that his government had inherited.

There are various opinions about what happened then, including some scathing verdicts about George Papandreou. Frankly, as an unbiased observer, it seemed to me that he was one of that rare breed, an honest politician. He told his country how bad things were, declared that there would need to be some draconian measures taken to try and fix the problem and then went to the country again owing to all the cries of no confidence in him. These cries seemed to me to be a result of people not liking the truth when they heard it. I heard a speech that he gave when he'd not been in power for long. In it he said, in essence,

"I'm going to do what's right for the country, no matter whether it's popular or not, no matter what it may mean for my position as Prime Minister, or indeed my political career. I'm going to do what needs to be done and it's going to hurt all of us."

Result? In the ensuing election he was voted out. Then came a "government of national unity" that was anything but. Then Mr. Samaras, the new leader of the New Democracy party was asked to form a government, also a coalition, then came the Syriza era under Mr. Tsipras.

Just a postscript on George Papandreou and why I believe that my estimation of him is close to the mark. He served as Prime Minister of Greece from October 6, 2009 until November 11, 2011. As Prime Minister, he was at the forefront of the global financial crisis and through complex and difficult negotiations, he managed to avoid his country's bankruptcy, while also applying a series of structural reforms to modernize Greece. For this reason he was named as one of Foreign Policy magazine's Top 100 Global Thinkers in 2010 for "making the best of Greece's worst year." That, in my book, qualifies him for a positive legacy.

Syriza was elected on a "no more austerity" ticket, which just about sums up all that's wrong with democracy. I'd liken the situation to a family. Let's face it, there are many similarities. A country needs to live alongside its neighbours and trade with them. It needs to earn its living in the world and 'cut the coat according to the cloth'. No cloth means no coat.

Put it this way, a set of parents give their son £10 per week pocket money. Then the father loses his job. Now with only one income coming in they can barely pay the mortgage and scarcely feed the three of them from week to week. Dad and mum say to their son, "Son, we can no longer give you £10 per week while the economic situation is as it is. You'll have to make do with £4 until we see more money coming into the house, whenever that may be." The son says, "I'm not having this! I want my £10 and you'd better give it to me." Where's that £10 going to come from? It's simply not there. Mr. Tsipras was elected on a similar wave of the public's refusal to accept the reality of the situation. The public don't want to see their income reduced. That's understandable, of course. But if the country's budget is over-stretched, if the balance of payments is so seriously in the red, there isn't much any government can do about it.

Here is where I return to the "talk is cheap" analogy. It's so easy for a party to campaign with a raft of promises because these are mere words. The facts are that whatever Syriza promised, (we'll kick out the Troika, we'll stop reducing pensions, we'll do this and we'll do that…") it was never going to be able to deliver, but the public elected them because the'd been told what they wanted to hear. Going back to Mr. Papandreou, he told them the truth ("Son, it'll have to be £4 from now on") and the public didn't want to hear it.

Democracy is where millions of people, largely ignorant of the facts, make decisions based upon their own desire not to see their pocket money reduced. Of course one should have sympathy for the son in the illustration and for the public in cash-strapped Greece. The facts, however, are harsh and the reality clear – everyone in the country will have to suffer fiscally for many years, possibly for some peoples' lifetimes, before the country is back on its feet, if it ever will be. If a child runs the family home, then disaster is the sure and only result in the end.

I get asked all the time, "How has the crisis affected you?" Lots of people also like to opine before even asking. That's why the numbers of people from northern Europe taking their summer holidays in Greece dropped once "austerity" kicked in. Vastly over-exaggerated stories about conditions here in Greece were circulated in the media in the UK, Germany, Poland, Scandinavia etc. - all the countries which form the backbone of the Greek tourism industry.

For instance, as a part time job I do a few excursions during the summer season. Without exception, every week for the past few years, especially soon after the news broke about how bad things were financially for Greece, I've found myself having the same conversation with guests from those countries referred to above. Usually my guests are die-hard Grecophiles who will come to Greece whatever happens because they love the country. They are usually sensible enough to see through all the hyped-up lies in the media. Yet so many of them have said to me,

"Our friends back home were horrified when we told them we were coming to Greece. They said things like 'You're going THERE? Is it SAFE? Surely there's no money in the Bank ATMs, no food in the hotels and tavernas, widespread begging on the streets, crime and violence everywhere."

I'm not exaggerating. Repeat visitors have told me how, when they got home from the previous holiday here on Rhodes, their neighbours, workmates or family said things like "Aren't you glad to be back home. It must have been awful for you."

OK, so it's a little different on the islands from the cities and the mainland, but all the same, my wife and I spent three days staying at a hotel slap bang in the centre of Athens in July 2014 and still we felt it a safer city to walk around at night than London. You know what a *perip'tero* is, its one of those kiosks that sells newspapers, drinks, confectionery and cigarettes and they're to be found along pavements all over Greece. We walked back from

Monastira'ki to our hotel, which was situated on the street that leads from Omonia Square to Syntagma (you can't get much more downtown that that) after midnight and those kiosks were closed for the night. Most of them have wooden eaves around which are hung the current copies of newspapers and magazine, attached to a string with wooden clothes pegs. As we walked home in the streets the shutters on the two or three perip'tera that we passed were rolled down, but the papers and magazines had been left on those pegs for the night. With no wish to denigrate my home country (and hopefully avoid kneejerk comments from UK readers), I can't see anyone doing such a thing there. Those periodicals would have been trashed, stolen or possibly set alight.

On the islands the vast majority of tourists who *have* decided to come for their holidays will tell you that it was as enjoyable as ever. The sunshine is still the same, the cuisine is the same, the welcoming people are the same and the scenery too. For many people on holiday, if they didn't know there was a crisis, they'd probably never have guessed.

As for us ex-pats living here, each must tell his or her own story. In our case the only appreciable effect that the financial crisis has had on us has been the cost of fuelling up the car. When we arrived in August 2005, petrol (OK... gasoline, guys) was about 85 cents per litre. That translated into around 60p in the UK, where it was selling for more like 90p. So in effect we were paying 60% of the UK price for our petrol. Today, in December 2016 we're probably paying 120% of what we'd be paying in the UK. Of course we have Greek friends who are on pensions who have seen their income cut by 40%. We have friends working in the tourism industry, especially those working in hotels, who have been made to wait for their wages for months at a time.

As for that last fact, I could be quite wrong, but I see it as the greedy hotel owners using the financial crisis as an excuse. The hotels to this day are still doing a roaring trade and the cash is flowing in thick and fast. Too many lowly staff (room cleaners, bar staff, waiters and waitresses) have been paid perhaps for the first month or two of the season, say May and June, then been told that they can't be paid until the end of the season or even later. It's scandalous and puts these hardworking people under extreme financial duress. Many of these folk are Albanians or Bulgarians and live in rented accommodation. By the time the season ends, they are several months behind with their rent and have been borrowing money to do their food shopping. They haven't been able to pay their electricity bills. Yet all the time they cheerfully serve the hotel guests as these laze around the pools and eat and drink to their heart's content in complete ignorance regarding what the staff who serve them are enduring.

At one hotel near us here in Kiotari, a couple of seasons ago an Albanian friend of ours organised a staff walk-out during September. None of the waged staff had received a bean since the end of June and they were desperate. In Rhodes town there is even reputed to be a union representing hotel workers, but for all the good it does it may as well be selling *souvlaki*.

What did the hotel management do? They sacked all the strikers with immediate effect and hired new ones. There are that many people out there willing to work in such conditions. In fact, our friend told us that he was owed a couple of thousand Euros when he was fired. He eventually got called into the hotel in November and told he'd have to accept 900 or nothing. That was the first actual income he'd received since the end of June. On top of that, each time he applied for a job for the following season he discovered that the hotel owners and management had been circulating his name to ensure that he didn't get hired. He has a wife and two children under ten by the way.

Eventually a restaurateur in Pefkos gave him a job, but not until he'd had to beg to be given the chance to prove what a good worker he was. Whilst my sister and her husband were out here staying with us we went out to eat there and saw for ourselves just how good our friend was at his job. He was the one smiling and laughing with the guests, while it was all the owner could do to acknowledge a "good evening" from his guests with a grunt.

Returning to politics then, as is par for the course, after 23 months in government Syriza is now being called a bunch of liars and Alexis Tsipras a betrayer. He got in on a wave of bravado. He was going to tell Europe what was what. Greece wasn't going to be bullied. Greece wasn't going to kow tow. After a visit or two to Brussels he and his finance minister at the time, Mr. Varifocals, sorry Varoufakis, soon got their reality check and discovered what life was like in the real world. The compromises that the PM agreed were too much for Yanis Varoufakis, who subsequently resigned. Give the man his due, he wanted to stick to his principles, something that most politicians find it simply impossible to do.

Where will Greece be in five years time, ten years time? The only thing I can say, in my humble, layman's opinion is this: Greece needs tourists, so please come.

5. Electric Shocks

Growing up in the UK, living one's first five decades and more there, one gets used to the modern conveniences. I don't think I ever came within a hundred yards of a portable electricity generator during my whole life in the UK. I knew that builders used them, of course, plus I could have probably described what your average modern diesel or petrol-powered generator looks like. I couldn't have told you how big they are or what level of noise they make though.

True, I'd seen those industrial jobs, the ones that are all panelled in and have two wheels and a tow-bar. You'd occasionally see one beside the road if it was perhaps powering temporary traffic lights on a stretch of road that was being dug up …again. That was about as far as my experience of portable generators went.

Moving out here from a UK home that had hot and cold running water and a steady 240v supply from the extremely reliable "national grid" (do they still call it that in these post-Thatcher days of privatisation?) you could say we'd gone soft. Mains sewerage too was something we'd become used to. When I was a kid in the fifties we had lived in Tunley, a small village six miles outside of Bath and at that house we'd had a cess-pit. Once we moved into Bath when I was about ten though, it was mains sewerage all the way. My days of seeing the huge tanker turn up and run its great smelly pipes snaking all the way down the length of the back garden were well and truly over.

So I thought.

Our home here on Rhodes was to be a brand new build. Our close friends John and Wendy were having it built with a separate wing for us to live in so that we'd have a permanent home and they'd have a holiday villa with a nicely manicured garden and someone on the spot to pay the bills for them and keep an eye on the place. In the UK a new build would conjure up in the minds of those planning to live in it all the latest conveniences and a spick and span building devoid of all those annoying problems that older properties often plague you with. Rising damp, rotting window frames, old leaky plumbing and an electrical system that was perhaps in need of a complete re-wire, all such things would not be expected in a brand new building.

The house out here was due for completion (already a revised date!) early in 2005. When we learned that it was behind schedule we weren't unduly concerned, until we began receiving regular bulletins from John and Wendy, who in turn were getting them from the builder, that were putting the completion date back, back, and then back some more. In the end John told the builder, "It had better be fit for purpose by the third week of August, something like ten months after the original completion date, because we're arriving. John and Yvonne [Maria, see my website: **http://johnphilipmanuel.wixsite.com/works/about1**] are going to be moving in and Wendy and I are going to have at least one holiday there before the summer season ends. Plus we have an MPV full of stuff to install and a jetRIB hitched on the back to park up outside."

Reluctantly the builder accepted that we'd be arriving on August 23rd and so we made plans for the journey in earnest. Most of the details about the overland (and sea) trip were related in the first memoir book in the "*Ramblings From Rhodes*" series, "*Feta Compli!*".

So, when our two vehicles (and a jetRIB on a trailer) drove up the dusty track to the house on the morning of August 23rd 2005, we foolishly expected to find a grand immaculate villa, garden cleared of builders' rubbish and perimeter fence all complete. Let's face it, in the UK you don't normally expect to move into a house which doesn't yet have a complete roof, do you?

What we found was truly daunting. OK, so the actual roof is a concrete slab, so at least the rooms weren't open to the air from above, but on top of the slab there was a wooden frame to support a pitched, terracotta-tiled roof, none of which was yet in evidence. There was no perimeter fence or wall whatsoever surrounding the four thousand square metre plot and there was rubbish everywhere. The drive was still compacted dirt, there was an old yellow Mercedes van parked up a few metres from our side of the house, its tyres all flat, which the tiny team of builders were using as their on-site toolshed, there were wooden pallets everywhere stacked high with ceramic tiles and roof tiles, there was only a concrete 'screed' floor on the terrace, or courtyard in the front of the house and no mains electricity.

The pressure in the water taps inside the house was lamentable, owing to the fact that the 'head' creating what little pressure there was consisted of a large translucent white PVC tank on the bank behind the house, barely higher than the roof. Our bedroom had a gaping metre-wide hole in its ceiling because one of the water pipes snaking above the plasterboard had sprung a leak and the stain on the bedroom floor beneath it bore witness to the fact. The builder had repaired the leak, but it had begun 'sweating' again and thus it was on his 'to do' list to try and fix it for a second time. There were air-conditioning units - not, however, on the walls but still looking snug, still unpacked in their cardboard boxes in the near 40ºC heat of an August Rhodes day. No mains electricity means no air-conditioning, since it's apparently illegal to install air-con in a property that doesn't have a proper electricity supply.

After the builder had shown us around and listed all the problems we were about to be living with, he introduced us to 'old-faithful', his ancient electricity generator with a woefully small fuel tank that, if you wanted to run it during daylight hours non-stop, would necessitate a refill every two or three hours. Much of the story regarding how we waited three months for mains electricity to be brought up the kilometre of valley from the main road to the villa is also recounted in *"Feta Compli!"*, so I needn't go into it here.

The old generator with the inadequate fuel tank was eventually replaced after a couple of weeks with a new one, all shiny yellow panelling and dials and knobs and stuff on the side. We then had the luxury of only having to fuel it up once per day. So I'd be out there as the weather began to break at the crack of dawn every morning week after week pouring diesel fuel from a huge rectangular PVC barrel into the ridiculously-positioned filler cap which, instead of being at the side for ease of reaching and pouring, was slap-bang in the middle of the machine's top, a horizontal rectangular panel about three feet by two.

Of course, the new generator conked out after a while and almost caught fire, which meant we had to return to old-faithful while it was being fixed. When I think back on all of this now it seems a lot longer than a few months that we had to contend with this situation.

When, almost three months to the day after we'd arrived, the Greek electricity company DEH finally switched us on, the relief was almost rapturous. It overwhelmed us and for quite a while afterwards I was still waking at the crack of dawn and contemplating that thirty metre walk over to the "genny" to fuel it up for another day. No more would I be spilling diesel in the back of our newly procured Suzuki Swift (ex-hire car, of course) after lugging that PVC drum, barrel or whatever you'd have called it, to the local filling station and back. No more would we be living with the constant drone of the generator's engine every waking minute, and struggling to visit the bathroom in the wee hours with a torch to give us a bit of light.

OK, so we still had to jump around in the shower to get wet enough to wash, but at least now we'd be able to go to the loo at three o'clock in the morning and see what we're doing by simply flicking the light-switch. I found myself gazing at the metre out there on its concrete obelisk, just savouring the fact that it actually existed. I'd watch that little metal wheel revolving, waiting for that black section to reappear as a reassurance that it was actually doing the job.

The honeymoon soon ended. Funny isn't it, but even with the droning throb of the diesel generator plaguing our ears all day long, at least I knew that as long as I could hear that noise our router was working, we had internet, the cooker could cook and the lights, when necessary, could illuminate the interior of the building. You could plug in the iron, or your hi fi, and it would become fit for purpose. I could play my Rory Gallagher or Stevie Ray Vaughan. My laptop would charge up.

Once we were connected to the mains the power cuts began. I believe that nowadays for some ridiculous reason they call them 'outages' in the UK or USA, right? Whatever you call it, it's still a power cut. Just when we thought it was safe to assume we had light and we could watch TV of an evening, those lovely folk at the Rhodes power station would plunge us into darkness. Just when I was trying to send files mid-morning over what was at the time still a dial-up internet account, a power cut would interrupt the transfer. As mentioned also in one of the *"Ramblings"* books, I accepted the advice that I was soon offered after arriving out here to buy a battery back-up anti-surge device. This at least meant that I could work on for twenty minutes or so when the power went down if I really had a screamer on, but the power would often be off for hours at a time, so the battery back-up didn't profit me all that much.

There was no pattern to it, it was a fact of life. Whenever we who were used to living in the modern world would talk to the builder about such things, he'd reply with a heavy dose of stoicism, "Welcome to Greece."

Back in the UK you'd never see glass-reservoired oil lamps sitting on top of someone's modern kitchen wall-unit. You'd never open the cupboard under the kitchen sink and see a plastic bottle of lamp oil in there, now would you? Here, every supermarket sells such things. We were soon sporting three oil lamps in our lounge and always kept a supply (still do, old habits…) of oil at the ready. I've lost count of the times when I decided that our lounge resembled a scene from an old Western movie, the only light available emanating from oil lamps sitting on the tables. All we needed to complete the picture was a woman with an off-the-shoulder dress and a few feathers in her hair draping herself over the chair behind me while I dealt the poker cards.

For the first couple of years we were living here the electricity would also regularly cut out at around 8.20pm, slap-bang in the middle of *Tis Metritis*, our favourite TV quiz show of the time, hosted by Spiro Papadopoulos. We had a British friend down the road who was married to a Greek woman from Asklipio. He was a retired civil engineer and assured me that he knew exactly why the power was regularly going off at the same time every evening. Once we got used to it we'd know that it was only going to be off at that time for ten to fifteen minutes. The reason for this brief 'outage', Bill told us, was that the workers in the diesel-fuelled power station were powering up the second generator to run its shift, and powering down the first, but they could never get the timing right for the second to come on-line before the first had powered down. Result, the whole island would experience a short period of 'down-time'.

Now, I don't have any idea if this was a logical explanation, but Bill assured us that he was in the habit of regularly calling DEH on the phone to give them a piece of his civil engineering mind about how doltish the power station staff were.

Power cuts during the day time were another thing altogether. Whenever there was work to be done on the lines, or perhaps a new construction project needing to be connected, the line engineers would turn off a swathe of the island's inhabitants while they did the job, with no warning. If it was a domestic house or two, maybe we'd be lucky and lose power for half an hour, maybe slightly more. If, though, there were new poles and cables going in somewhere, we could say goodbye to a cup of coffee or a pot of tea for hours at a time. For the first few years power cuts were so 'normal' that you could expect the electricity to be off at least once every day for anything from an hour to six hours, although anything over two was mercifully quite rare.

As the years have passed the number of solar energy 'farms' has increased rapidly and I'm inclined to believe that this is the primary reason for the much more reliable electricity supply that we now experience. There are still power cuts, but nowhere near as often or for such long periods as they were during the first two or three years we were here.

These solar energy farms, which display long lines of mirrored panels soaking up the sunshine and converting all that light into electrical energy are not the prettiest things to view in the countryside, but at least they don't make a noise, they don't emit greenhouse gases and they do add to the amount of power generated on the island as a whole. When we first got here, we very soon heard about the debate over the need for a new power station. While the debate raged on, the power cuts did too. It seems that there was much argument over where to build the new one. Everyone agreed that a new power station was a necessity, but the debate was hot and edgy about whose land it should eventually be built on.

Finally, in 2013 work began, much to the chagrin of the "Save Prassonissi" campaign, who had us all believing that the rather beautiful island which is joined to the far southern tip of 'mainland' of Rhodes by an hourglass shaped strand of sand, would be ruined. It's always a swings and roundabouts situation this issue of preservation of the natural environment. I mean, who of us would prefer to return to the age when you had to trim an oil or gas lamp to get any light or heat once the sun has gone down? Who of us now would happily do without his or her electronic device and the convenience of being able to plug in its charger? Yet none of us wants to see wanton destruction of the natural world either.

Having been down to Prassonissi on several occasions since the construction of the new plant began several years ago now, I can only say that in my opinion they've done a pretty good job of selecting the location. For starters, the countryside as you drive from the village of Kattavia down to Prassonissi isn't the most picturesque of vistas anyway, criss-crossed as it is with tank tracks because vast swathes of it are used for military manoeuvres on a regular basis. It's for this reason that my wife and I dubbed the area "Salisbury Plain", since in the UK that's where the landscape is very similar. Salisbury Plain has long been turned over largely to military use and there, as in the area between Kattavia and Prassonissi, you see long scars of tank tracks all over the hillsides of the once spectacular plain.

The new power station is tucked into a hollow and, once you've driven past it (and the road is some distance from the actual installation anyway), you very soon lose it behind a hillside and, once you get to Prassonissi, you'd never even know it was there at all. Ask many locals about whether they think it ought to be built and most will respond with a very positive "Yes, of course. It will not only meet the ever increasing demand placed on the electrical grid here on Rhodes by tourism development, but it will also provide much-needed employment in the region." OK, so the locals may not say it with such erudition.

For the last few years we've even had a fairly fast broadband connection here in the south of the island too, albeit with slightly patchy coverage. All in all though, we do seem to be finally living in something resembling the modern world. We even have digital TV – now and then. It's very weather and season-dependent. Ah well, you win some you lose some, as is the case with the TV channels.

Not that you won't still see portable generators dotted about the place though. There are still so many houses suffering with legality issues that they can't get mains electricity connected anyway, and thus they rely on a generator to keep their beers cold in the fridge.

Among other things, of course.

The power surges are something else you need to be aware of living here. In the past few years things have improved immeasurably, but time was when power surges were a regular occurrence and you kept hearing of people whose computers had been toasted or their TV had blown up. We lost our first fridge-freezer owing to power surges. It was a Bosch, and we'd paid handsomely for it when we'd first arrived here. Unfortunately, only after it had burnt out its circuitry for the second time did we find out about those little individual surge-protectors that you can plug into each wall socket. They only cost three or four Euros too. The first time the thing went wrong it was still under warranty and the store where we'd bought it sent an engineer out to look at it. In this case we were well impressed with the service. The store offered us a replacement while the little piece of circuitry that had blown was on order, but we were able to make use of our landlords' one next door because it was winter time and they weren't using theirs.

Light bulbs are another thing you get used to replacing more often here than in the UK. Of course, now they're all being turned over to the low-energy power-saving type, but the run-of-the-mill light bulbs we used when we first came here blew so often that it was an essential to have a dozen or so stashed in a cupboard if we were to stand a chance of not being plunged into darkness at night owing to so many bulbs having blown.

The last time I'd had anything to do with candles in the UK was decades ago when I last went into a church. Out here a box of candles was another essential to have stored under your kitchen sink.

I have to say, though, that in the past year or two the *'revma'* has been much more reliable. *'Revma'* is the word used when Greeks are discussing their power supply. It literally translates as 'current' or 'stream', but is universally used when the conversation revolves around electricity.

"Do you have *revma?*" Someone will ask you if the power supply is down. Well, it's much more rare nowadays to hear such a question because, finally, after many years of living with regular and often prolonged cuts to one's *revma*, I have to admit that the power supply is becoming almost as reliable as it was in the UK.

Time was when you could be doing the ironing, boiling the kettle, cooking something in the oven, charging your phone, computer or tablet, watching TV and suddenly that dreaded silence would descend upon the house as everything that was plugged into a socket fell into inactivity. If it happened after dark you'd have to have remembered not to close your blinds completely or else you'd be in absolute darkness, which meant that if you hadn't had the foresight to have a torch, lighter or box of matches to hand, then you'd soon be nursing a stubbed toe, clearing up some broken glass or wondering if the cat ought to be taken to the vet to check out whether the injury was life-threatening or not.

Yes, in Greece, at least here on Rhodes, we're almost in the 21st century at last.

I've even recently taken 'a portable generator' off my wish-list of things to save up for.

Now that's progress.

6. Paperwork

In the UK we were used to everything being computer-based. We used to have a string of Direct Debits going out of our bank account every month that was long enough to wrap up a decent sized horse. I don't know why a horse, it was the first thing that came to mind when I was trying to think up a clever and witty example. Another failure there then.

When I used to examine our bank statement, on-line of course, even back in 2005, the majority of the transactions it showed in any calendar month were these wretched DDs. Such was life in British society. Mortgage, life insurance, insurance on the mortgage, Insurance on the house and contents, electricity, gas, water, council tax, the list was endless. I have to admit that it did depress one somewhat looking at how much disposable we had left as income out of what had gone in once all the Debits had flown the cash right out again.

But at least everything was streamlined. I could honestly say that I can't remember the last time I queued up anywhere to pay a bill when we lived in South Wales. Never went into the bank any more, never went to any offices or stores to wait for ages and hand over some cash to a person who made it very evident from their demeanour that they'd rather be anywhere but where they were and viewed all of us public, who paid their salaries, with total disdain.

No, all I had to do was slave away month on month and then read my life story in columns on my PC screen before deciding that I'd maybe give it another month before I decided to top myself.

Here? Yes, well, here things are just a tad different. Where does one even start? Well, tax numbers would be the logical place. You can't really begin to function here in Greece until you have a tax number. In order to obtain it you must take a clutch of paperwork along to the main tax office which in our case is an hour's drive away on the outskirts of Rhodes town. The only nice thing about the tax office is the fact that it stands only a couple of hundred metres from the sea and therefore ought to have a view. Most of the time you're inside the building however, you don't. You could be anywhere and usually wished you were.

As every year passes the goalposts change of course. When we bit the bullet and queued up for our tax numbers you needed your birth certificate, your marriage certificate, your passport, your Greek bank account passbook (in order to show a required minimum balance if I remember correctly, which I probably don't because we did this eleven years ago now, but you get the general picture) and your inside leg measurement. My memory's sketchy on that last one. Maybe it was your waist.

Not only did you need all those things, you also had to have anything that originated from the UK translated into Greek and rubber-stamped to show that the translation had been done by a lawyer. There, you see, the first expense that you probably didn't foresee. We certainly didn't. After having shelled out fifty Euros to the lawyer who'd handled the purchase of the property for our landlords John and Wendy, so that we could waltz along to the tax office with one A4 sheet of paper with hardly enough words on it to make a limerick work, we ...well, we waltzed along to the tax office.

Oh, and don't think for a moment that there was any piece of paper remotely resembling a bill or receipt to show that we'd paid the lawyer anything.

Once you've queued up a few stairwells, along a couple of windowless corridors and around a clutch of offices with large glass screens separating the employees from the terminally bored public, you eventually see the desk you're queuing for coming into view. It's about now that you realise that your bladder wasn't expecting to go this long without being relieved and you start sweating because if you leave your place in the queue you know it'll be another two or three hours before you get back to the same spot you're at. You've fought long and hard for this so you simply decide that a cyst or perhaps the odd kidney stone isn't life-threatening and you stick it out. Boy did we run fast once we'd got our tax numbers done though. You're given your tax number on, guess what, an A4 sheet of photocopier paper and you'll be keeping it somewhere safe for a very long time. You're going to need to show it pretty often during your first few months here.

Also, to get it sorted, you have to give the clerk your mother's maiden name and your father's first names. It's not only the government that requires such information. Even now our bank pass book (yes, even with a regular account they still use pass books) shows my name as John Philip Kenneth (my dad's name) Manuel. I have a few documents that show both of my dad's first names too.

Once you have your tax number you're motoring. Well, actually, you're not because you can't buy a car without also showing your residency permit. Now, as I write this the hot potato is Brexit, but in 2005 the UK was well and truly part of the EU and according to EU law residency permits aren't a requirement. Free movement of citizens and labour and all that stuff. Forget it. Here you still can't buy a car, a house or quite a few other things if you can't produce the permit. If, for example, you want to work over here, you had at one time to exchange the residency permit for a work permit. At least that's now changed, as I have a permit that covers both.

When we first applied for our residency permits, however, it entailed taking along all the same paperwork that you needed for your tax number, together with your newly acquired tax number (A4 photocopied sheet) plus a couple of passport type photos to the nearest police station. Here, often as not, the staff would have a good laugh (although not overtly) giving newly-arrived ex-pats the runaround. Well, let's face it, life as a police officer on a Greek island can be pretty dull. They need something to make them feel life's worth living. Mind you, they do all have a frappé on the go most of the time.

The scenario would go something like this:

You walk into the police station. There's a desk in the lobby with one old-fashioned dial-type telephone on it. It's grey. There's no one behind the desk, but you can see through a doorway to the side another desk and there's a uniformed officer sitting on it chatting up a uniformed female officer. They both hold a frappé in one hand and a cigarette in the other. You cough to get their attention, whereupon the male policeman sitting on the desk casts a glance your way and waves a hand as if to say, "Take a seat. I'll be out in an hour or so."

He lies. It's only 45 minutes and he comes out to ask what you're after. You tell him you need to obtain your residency permits and he points toward another doorway and says,

"You need to see *Kyrio* Panayioti. He's in there."

You make as if to go "in there" and the officer extends a preventative hand while adding, "But he doesn't work today. Tomorrow he is here. After eleven o'clock."

Next day at eleven sharp you go back. After all, it's only half an hour's drive from home. Each way. You make as if to go into Panayioti's office and another young officer asks you what you're doing. You explain that you want to obtain residency permits. They reply,

"Kyrios Panayiotis will be here soon."

"But we were told that he starts at eleven," you hopefully return.

"He comes when he comes. You must wait," he says, pointing you at the same seats you spent three quarters of an hour in yesterday.

Half an hour later a big bloke in leathers, still wearing a full-face crash helmet with blacked out visor, walks in. Glancing out through the dusty window you see a huge motorcycle parked outside. Hmm, you're thinking, wonder what he's done. Maybe had an accident, or perhaps he needs to report in, like to a probation officer or something. No, no no. You've just had your first glimpse of Panayioti, the non-uniformed officer who, among other stuff, processes (at his leisure, you're soon to discover) residency permits for foreigners.

He ignores you and walks straight into his office. In there he removes his helmet and places it on a shelf behind his desk, messes around with a whole bunch of A4 photocopied pieces of paper in front of him and then picks up his phone. He's unbuttoned his leather biking jacket to reveal a Motorhead t-shirt underneath. While you stare hopefully in his direction he makes sure to avoid all eye contact until a young man trots in through the front door carrying a fresh frappé and places it on Panayioti's desk. That was what he was doing with his phone then.

Finally, he looks out at you and waves you in, an expression not dissimilar from the one Hannibal Lecter may have worn while viewing his next victim, or should I say roast dinner, on his face.

You go in and tell him you want to apply for residency permits. He says (with a degree of glee) that you're going to need this, this, this and a few of those plus some passport photos before he can begin to process your permits. He's visibly crestfallen when you triumphantly produce all the required paperwork and drop it rather smugly on the desk between you for him to examine.

After he's passed a couple of A4 photocopied sheets across the desk for you to fill in, which takes you about fifteen minutes because the questions are all in Greek and you probably don't understand most, or indeed any of them, he shows you where to sign. Here, here, here and, also here.

"Is that it?" You ask after signing, ever the optimist.

"You come back next Tuesday." He replies.

"Next Tuesday? We can't have them now then?"

"Next Tuesday. They'll be here. You come then." By his tone of voice you know that the conversation's over and it's time to leave.

He sips his frappé contentedly as you walk out the door.

The following Tuesday, in you walk, thankful that this is hopefully your last visit to the police station for a very long while. The young officer who 'greeted' you the first time you came in asks what you want. Short memory, or what?

"We've come for our residency permits." you reply.

He comes back with "Kyrios Panayiotis isn't here today."

"But he told us to come today. It's Tuesday. He said to come to…"

"His schedule changes. Thursday he is here. You must to come then."

At this point you're toying with the idea of losing it. The problem is, if you do, there's only one outcome possible and it isn't going to be the one you'd be happy with.

Two days later, in you walk and you're incredibly relieved to have noticed Panayioti's big bike outside. You don't bother to wait for an invitation, but walk straight into his office, where he makes sure not to raise his head to acknowledge your presence. Such a clever way of establishing who has dominance in this situation. You are, however, excited to see that he is shuffling through a stack of A4 photocopies, all of which have A5 pale green cards paper-clipped to them.

Things are looking up. Not for long though. When he's decided that you're sufficiently humiliated, he looks up and gestures with a hand for you to sit down.

"Have our permits come?" You enquire, trying with a superhuman strength you never knew you had until now to remain civil and respectful.

"Name?" He asks. By now you are coming to realise that loquaciousness isn't one of his stand-out qualities. You tell him and he immediately shakes his head.

"We are waiting for a new supply of cards. You have to give me a week or two, sorry." Sorry is one thing he ain't. Take it from me.

As you walk out it's difficult not to imagine the three or four staff within sharing a good belly laugh at your expense.

All the foregoing is no exaggeration. It's how it went for us. What was truly dismaying and almost reduced me to tears was the realisation that, once we'd walked out with our permits, on reading them we discovered that the initial permit you'd received back then only lasted for six months. After that if you still wanted to stay they'd give you a permanent one.

Six months down the line back we went and, although things progressed just a little more smoothly this time, we almost screamed with frustration to see that our new permits still had a six month expiry date on them. Now go on, tell me they weren't having us on, giving us the runaround.

As it happened in our case, we let the permits lapse long after their expiry dates because we'd already bought the car and done a few other things that required that one show one's permit. So, after four or five years, when we realised that to do any work on a legal basis, or to change the car, we were going to to have to show valid permits, we steeled ourselves for a repeat performance.

It's amazing how speaking Greek changes everything. By the time we went in for our permanent work permits we were both much more proficient in speaking the language. My wife always was ahead of me, but although she has Greek blood, she'd been brought up without speaking Greek around the house owing to the blinkered thinking of her British father, so she too struggled in the beginning.

This time we were treated with smiles and instantly granted our new and thankfully permanent residency/work permits. I know a lot of Ex-pats who always excuse their failure to learn Greek with the stock response that "they always talk back to you in English anyway." I'm here to tell you that this isn't because they don't want foreigners to learn Greek, it's because they simply want to practice their English. I've had so many conversations over the years with ex-pats who tell me their horror stories about the trouble they've had with uncooperative bank staff, government officials and the like in parallel situations to ours where things have gone smoothly for us that I've only been able to sympathise with them in word, because our experience has been totally different since we became able to converse in Greek.

There are still folk out here who haven't applied for permits. They'll resolutely stick to the mantra that according to European law they are not required. That's as maybe, but you still can't buy a car or do quite a few other things if you don't have one. Not legally anyway.

So, now we had our tax numbers and our residency/work permits, surely it would be plain sailing from here on in. In September 2009 the government brought in a new requirement for all residents of the country, Greek or foreign. Everyone had to register for an AMKA number. It's a social security number that one had to obtain by visiting the nearest KEP office. What's KEP in Greece? It's the national network of Citizens Service Centres, a bit like the Citizen's Advice Bureau in the UK, but with more powers.

You need to visit a KEP office for a number of legal reasons. When we bought our first car I didn't have to go there. I bought it from a local car hire guy who's since proven to be a good friend and he helped me through the whole process. The paperwork in Greece for buying or selling a car is hugely cumbersome and thoroughly irritating. In the UK we had the DVLA, the Driver and Vehicle Licensing Authority, that issues all vehicle registration documents. Every vehicle comes with the DVLA document (we used to call it the log book in the old days, because it did indeed supersede a real old-fashioned log book as proof of who is the keeper of the vehicle) and when you change the vehicle you just fill out the new owner's details at the bottom of the document, tear it off and mail it to the DVLA. The new owner receives a new document showing them to be the vehicle's legal keeper and you receive one for your newly acquired car too. Simple.

Oh boy. Oh boy! When it came time to change our car here I really discovered how convoluted the whole affair is. Trying hard not to go off at too many tangents or follow any red herrings, here is what you have to do.

Firstly, you do have an accountant don't you? No? Really? Let's get this bit straight from the off. If you live in Greece and own a car, you have to have an accountant. You don't have to be a property owner. If you have a car you need an accountant. You may not earn enough to pay tax, but the government nevertheless requires that you fill in an annual tax return and they spend millions on staff, hard and software and unnecessary forms processing tax returns from which they garner no income whatsoever.

The only winners are the accountants. That's why almost every village has at least one. We have to hand over fifty Euros each year to ours. Now that we've finally sorted out all the various anomalies in our situation, which would extend the length of this chapter by several hundred percent were I to try and explain it all here, what it entails is a visit every May/June to his office, where he checks that nothing in our situation has changed, prints out a form for me to sign and submits our return on line. Yes I know, it is amazing isn't it, but at least in the last few years this has become possible. Phew. Welcome to the twenty-first century, Greece.

So, for about fifteen minutes work he earns fifty Euros. Multiply that by all the local folk who have to use his services and you see what I mean about the accountants being the winners. Mind you, I don't envy them one thing. The regulations change every year without fail. Sometimes several times during a tax year. Last time I went in to have our return processed he showed me the guidebook that the government issues for accountants. It was like a telephone directory (remember those?) and he has to become familiar with it if he's to offer the correct advice to his clients, or indeed to process their returns legally. I still have bad dreams about homework from my schooldays, he still has to do his, with no end in sight.

It was my accountant who first alerted me to the legalities that I had to follow when I sold my old car and bought another. The process is something like this. Fix yourself a drink first, maybe…

When you agree a sale, or indeed a purchase, you need to visit the KEP office for some forms. Yes, you've guessed, they're A4 photocopied forms and they're called 'Solemn Statement' or something like that. There are several types of 'Solemn Statement' but there is one especially for selling and buying vehicles. Every vehicle also has a logbook, which is much more like the old ones we used to have in the UK than it is like the registration document that they have had for the past thirty years or so. The logbook is a four-page card that has to be kept in the vehicle at all times, along with the insurance documents. The logbook is clearly not something that can be computerised and …well, I'll come to that later.

I had to go to the KEP office with both the person I was selling my old car to and the person I was buying my next one from. All of us needed to fill out the 'Solemn Statements' in order to be able to give them to our accountants as proof of the transactions. Guess what, among other information you have to put on the solemn statement is your passport number and your tax and AMKA numbers. Oh, and my dad's name is on there too. You fill out two statements with the person you're selling to and another two with the person you're buying from. This is because you both need copies that can be rubber stamped, signed and dated by the clerk in the KEP office. Once you've done all that you have to get the logbook updated on the vehicle you're buying. This can also be done through the KEP organisation, although if you're able to drop into the KTEO (government vehicle testing stations are run by this organisation, it stands for *Kendro Techniko Elengho Ohimaton* – basically meaning Vehicle Inspection Centre) you can do it there too. You can't do it by post. Once I'd been into the KEP office down the road in Gennadi and filled out a form with the new details that needed to go on to the logbook of the car I was buying, I then had to wait while the old logbook was "sent off" and my new one arrived.

When I say "sent off", it rather involved the girl who works at the KEP office driving up to Rhodes town once a week with various paperwork, including any logbooks needing to be updated. I only found this out because, after having left the affair in the hands of the girl at the KEP office, a couple of days later I bumped into her while she was having a coffee in Gennadi square, during working hours of course.

I asked her, "Has my new logbook arrived yet?"

"Um, no," she replied, "I haven't had time to drive up to town with the paperwork. Had to go to a funeral this week." It seems she drives to town on the same day each week, but this particular week, as luck wouldn't have it, someone in the village had rather inconsiderately died and, since the whole village usually turns out for the funeral, she'd gone too, and it was on the day she usually goes to town. So she hadn't yet delivered the papers to the KTEO office for processing.

As you'll have gathered too, the logbook doesn't come directly in the post, it comes to the KEP office, brought back by the fair hand of the girl who works there. Pony express? Almost.

I only found out about the "solemn statement" when I told my accountant about eight months later that I'd changed the car.

"Do you have the statements?" he asked me, when I dropped by to see him do my tax return and extract his fifty Euros from me.

"Umm, what statement?"

"Well, you changed your car, so I'll need your statements showing the details of the sale and the purchase."

When I'd dropped into the KEP office about updating the logbook she hadn't said a word then, so I had no idea they were required, or that they even existed. Imagine, eight months after the old car was sold to a Bulgarian bloke who heard about the fact that I was selling it through a couple of mutual friends, I had to phone him and ask if he'd mind us taking a trip to a KEP office to sign these statements. Quite why he hadn't been bothered when he'd bought it wasn't any of my business. Looked pretty clear to me, though, that he didn't bother with an accountant. Not wise. I was amazed when he agreed. When we eventually got together and filled out the forms, if I remember right, it also involved a trip to the police station for them to rubber stamp, date and sign the statements too. The Bulgarian had to work and so I went alone. He never did come back to me about collecting his copy of the statement. It's probably still in my box of papers that I laughingly call my filing cabinet.

The woman I bought the 'new' car from had moved back to the UK and so I had to get her Greek accountant to sign her copies of our version of the statements by proxy.

I tell you, if you have a car out here and it's legal, keep the damn thing until it conks out for good.

At least when the government introduced the new AMKA numbers it could all be accomplished with one visit to the KEP office, amazingly.

The vehicle road tax system here is a bit daft too. Things have improved during the past few years though. At least nowadays you can renew your road tax on-line, as long as you can negotiate the government's website, which is in Greek. When we first arrived I was surprised to learn that, unlike in the UK, where road tax runs from the month during which you purchased the vehicle, here everyone has to renew their road tax for January 1st every year. Bureaucratically speaking – logjam city.

Back in 2005 I had no idea about this until the last week before Christmas, when I thought it best to ask someone how one renews the tax. I'd bought the car with a few months' tax still valid. In those days the fact that you had paid your road tax was made evident by a little blue sticker which everyone had to display on their windscreen. Seeing mine running out I called Taki, the bloke I'd bought the car from, and asked him how I should go about renewing the tax.

"Ah, yes, Johnny (I have yet to meet a Greek who can call me John, it's always Johnny), Since the Tax office and post offices are closed for quite a few days over the Christmas and New Year holidays, you'd be best advised to go to the tax office in Rhodes Town. If you don't renew it by the first week of January, there could be a hefty fine to pay."

Cue yet another tax office experience, much like the one we'd endured when obtaining our tax numbers just a few months before. Once again we were queuing up stairwells and along corridors, all kinds of paperwork clutched in our sweaty palms, until our bladders alerted us to the fact that we ought to be at last nearing the desk which was our goal. It looked to me as if everyone on Rhodes left it until the very last minute to renew their vehicle road tax. I vowed that 'd never do this again.

From the following year onwards, until a couple of years ago when the government finally abolished the windscreen stickers in favour of a simple form that you print out from the website and keep in the car, I made sure I'd paid my road tax renewal by the end of the first week of December, which meant I could do it in a local bank or post office. This past year, for the first time, I've done the whole thing on line, payment and all.

Finally things are improving. We appear to be getting somewhere. The whole system here is still, though, heavily dependent on A4 photocopied forms. I've said it before and I'll repeat it here, Greece may be in economic crisis, it may be difficult to keep a business going, but if you're into the manufacture of rubber stamps, you're probably doing very well thank you.

7. Legalities

It's not a pleasant subject this one. But, since I want to paint a complete picture, which means talking about the negatives along with the positives, this chapter might just be described as 'well into the negative column'. Sorry about that, but you wouldn't want to consider moving out here if you weren't armed with the complete picture.

It's hard, when I wrack my brain, to think of anyone we know who's moved out here and bought a property, who hasn't also bought a nightmare beyond belief. There is one couple, who we haven't seen in a while, who did buy way back on the early noughties and rented an apartment nearby throughout the duration of their build and, if I remember correctly from what Alf told me some years ago, things went fairly smoothly. He went to the building site at least once a week and sometimes more often, to take photographs of the entire progress of the build. He used a different lawyer from the one his builder used, a key factor.

What's the problem? Well, I can only say it as I see it, after having talked with ex-pats who've bought properties, usually off-plan before a sod was even turned, and that's how I'll present my take on the whole affair.

Where to start is also a problem. Right, well, there are loads of half-built properties all over Greece as anyone who comes here for their holidays will have noticed. Of course, some of these are actually completed homes and businesses and the only thing making them look unfinished is the ugly forest of 're-bars' sticking out of the roof. This, as I'm sure most people now know, was owing to a loophole in the building laws that allowed people not to pay the final tranche of tax on a new building because to all intents and purposes the occupiers could point upward when an inspector called to enquire as to where the money was and say:

"Well, would you look at that! The building's not completed yet. There's another floor to be added."

The inspector knew full well that the adding of another floor was never going to happen, but he couldn't prove it and the occupiers couldn't provide a date for completion and so the stalemate ensued and the government went without a few thousand Euros which was by rights due to it. A few years ago, now, they closed this loophole by placing a time limit for building to be finished. Once they exceeded that reasonable date, the tax was due whether the owners liked it or not. It has amused me now and again to see men up on flat roofs with grinders, cutting off those rusty, redundant re-bars that were never ever going to be used to anchor another storey.

There are also, of course, the empty concrete shells that are so unsightly and sadly all too common. I posted on my blog a couple of years back explaining that there are actually three reasons for this, two of which are perhaps acceptable, the other not so much so. For the whole story, check out my *"Ramblings From Rhodes"* blog and type "Shells" into the search field in the left hand column. You'll find there's a post called "Shells, But Not the Ones on the Beach" and it will reveal all. For the time being here though, I'll concentrate on the third and least attractive reason for these eyesores, property speculation.

Between the years 2000 and 2008 there was a bit of a boom in property sales to foreigners, mainly British, clamouring to get out to Greece and start living the dream. There were web-sites aplenty enticingly advertising that the people running them would not only provide eager buyers with the property they'd always dreamed of, but they'd guide the gullible through the whole process right down to the day they arrived out here, high-factor cream at the ready, for a life in the sun.

I say 'gullible', but I ought to qualify that. Frankly a lot of people who in their home country would be nothing like gullible could never have dreamed of the tricks that were being pulled over here and thus placed their confidence in scurrilous entrepreneurs who saw each and every British person as a walking ATM. They became gullible through simply not believing that what was about to happen to them could actually happen.

I've already referred briefly to the tax that needs to be paid on completion of a new property. I'm no expert and have virtually nil experience of the building industry back in the UK, where I came from, but I do know that out here each new build is liable to pay a sum of tax to the government at certain specified stages of the build, with the final payment becoming due on completion of the property, hence the old loophole about the re-bars.

For seven or eight years, there were speculators over here who were busy advertising in UK glossy magazines and the Sunday papers and finding clients who were desperate to start a new life. Back then you could buy a house that looked like it would cost, say, £300,000 in Britain, for the equivalent of half that in Euros. Bingo! There was no shortage of takers. What would the 'builders' do? Well, say you were buying your dream home here on Rhodes and the time came finally for you to pack up the rest of your belongings, ship them over in a container and fly out here to be handed the keys to your wonderful new villa, no doubt with a pool. That's because what you were saving in comparative property prices made it more than do-able to have a pool. After all, wasn't that what the high life required?

You'd have transferred your final payment to your 'builder', which of course contained several thousand Euros in tax which he would have to pass on to the government. The only trouble was, rather than hand perhaps 10,000 to the tax man, the 'builder' thought, 'I'll use that to lay another concrete base for the next property that I'm going to sell. Once I get the downpayment on that, then I'll pay the tax (on your property) to the government. No sweat. Aren't I clever?' He would be wrong though, eventually.

In 2008, when the world's financial bubble finally burst, everything changed overnight. All of a sudden the seemingly endless supply of foreigners eager to up sticks and move to Greece dried up. Within months there were formerly excellent glossy magazines about Greece which were printed and circulated in the UK going to the wall. I know, I wrote a few pieces for one of them and was sorely distressed when it went under and ceased publication. Ninety percent (only guessing, but it had to be something like that) of its advertising income came from Greek developers advertising to the folk in chilly Britain about their wonderful properties (not yet built of course) available at ridiculously cheap prices over here in hot, sunny Greece.

Say you had bought right at the end of the boom, right when the bubble burst. You would probably not have even been aware that the 'builder' hadn't actually paid your final tranche of building tax. After all, you'd paid it to him in good faith. Unbeknown to you, your 10,000 tax was now in concrete in the corner of some olive grove, about to languish there for years as the bottom dropped out of the market in spectacular fashion.

The first you'd know about it would be maybe a few years after you'd moved in. There would come a knock on your door and some official would be there to discuss the legalities of your property. This is where the fun begins. The official tells you that you still owe 10,000 completion tax on your house, plus interest. They also turn and point at your pool and say:

"Why have you a pool? There is no mention of a pool on the plans that were submitted for approval. There will be fines, the cost of a pool license [possibly a four-figure sum] plus one or two other charges that we can dream up."

Then they'll really get the taste for their job. They'll say they need to measure your house's footprint to be sure that it complies with architect's original drawings, they'll take photographs and measurements with their fancy instruments and finally advise you that your detached property isn't actually meant to be detached. The plans showed, and the law specifies, that your property ought to be linked in a row of three. You already know that all three in question are detached. Once they've taken all the measurements they tell you that your house ought to be 95 square metres and in fact it's been built to 105, so that will incur another fine. Your kitchen isn't where it ought to be and you should have a built-under garage, which the plans show ought to be where your kitchen is. The upstairs balconies are too big and the perimeter wall is in the wrong place. Oh, and if you think you've bought freehold, you haven't. In fact the three owners of the three properties actually own all three plots jointly. You don't own your plot all by yourselves, you're joint owners with the other two. This means that you won't be able to sell, even if and when you finally get your house legal, without the agreement of the other two owners. In effect it's one plot with three properties on it, three properties that should be linked and in fact aren't.

This above scenario is not a rare occurrence. It's virtually par for the course. Now, I have been placing parentheses around the word 'builder' as you may have noticed. This is because lots of British people have bought from people who simply had land which was surplus to requirements and thus they thought they'll sell it off and make a wad of cash. They'd employed dodgy workers to do the builds and lots of brown envelopes had flown around during the building process. Thus the civil engineers who were meant to check that your house was going up correctly and legally didn't need to come to the site in order to sign off the various stages of the build. A well-placed brown envelope here and there invalidated the need to actually make the inspection. Slam dunk.

Now, your initial reaction to all this dismaying news that looks liable to set you back anything up to another 20,000, is to remonstrate with the official and suggest that they go see the 'builder' you bought from.

"I paid that tax!!" You'd exclaim. "The builder received the money. It's him you want to be chasing, not us."

"Ah, well, I'm afraid that it's your name on the tax bill that's due, therefore it's you who are liable to pay it."

Quite how these 'builders' could get away with such sharp practice is beyond those of us from the UK, where we have such things as ombudsmen and various organisations to protect the buyer's interests. Out here you can't read the small print. You don't know the system. Dammit, why did you agree when the 'builder' suggested that you open a joint bank account with him, just so that the whole transfer of money thing would go smoothly and not delay the progress of the build? Yes, that's what many did. Plus he suggested that either signature would do to withdraw cash from the account, not both. Oh, and while we're about it, may as well use the same lawyer and the same accountant. Oh dear.

I know of one case where a UK ex-pat was awoken from his siesta one day to find bailiffs outside his door. They were there to evict him over a huge debt which his builder has run up with an electrician which hadn't been paid. This poor bloke had poured all his life's savings into his house on Rhodes and had no idea that his builder had then proceeded to use his house as collateral, since they shared a bank account. The 'builder' had defaulted on the debt, done a runner and left the poor British man living in a house that he thought he owned and yet discovered that now it belonged to the electrician, who had accepted the property in place of a cash repayment of what he was owed. In fact, the electrician was as in the dark as the British man, not having been aware, when the deal had been done for him to take over ownership of the property, that a poor ex-pat was living there labouring under the impression that it was his house. He had paid for it, after all.

The trouble is, and I hate to say it, the Greeks will close ranks. The problem of the *'fakelaki'* [brown envelope] culture is that civil engineers, bank officials, architects and a few others besides have often all been in on it, the only people in ignorance being the poor ex-pats who unwittingly bought a property that was entirely illegally built, and often to poor building standards too.

I know of several British couples who have paid their final tranche of building tax twice, yes twice, because the 'builder' was just too slippery to be caught when the unpaid tax came to light. Some, of course, simply don't have the money. Thus, some (even past retirement age) have had to find a job out here and slave away all through the summer season, when they thought they'd be sitting around their pool with a cool drink and a Jeffery Archer, to earn the money to pay back what they owe (even though they'd already paid it) over several years. That's not to mention all the fines on illegally built homes too.

Electricity is another minefield. In the UK, when a new house is built in goes the electricity meter. You buy the property and you contact the electricity company to agree on your moving in date. You start paying your bills. End of story.

Here, well, it's not quite so straightforward. When a property build is under way, the law states that a concrete obelisk has to be erected near the property's perimeter and the meter mounted on it so that it can be read without the reader having to enter the property. Each build also has to have a rough sign mounted at its perimeter too, displaying the number of the building permit. At this stage, if you're lucky and the build has gone according to plan, all the receipts have been kept and taxes paid, the meter may be fitted (inside a grey box, which is installed by one bloke, but not the same bloke who installs the meter. Don't ask me why this should be) and once connected you are on what's commonly known as 'builder's supply'.

Under the terms of 'builder's supply' the property has mains electricity, but only on a temporary contract, valid usually for a maximum of two years, after which the build ought to be finished and the property signed off as fit for habitation. At that point the electricity company sends an inspector out to look at the installation. If he's happy and all the relevant taxes have been paid and receipts for entire build rendered to your accountant for government inspection, then you can have it signed over to 'domestic tariff', which is considerably cheaper than 'builder's'.

Unfortunately for many ex-pats buying out here, there have been that many abnormalities with the paperwork on their property during the build, that they haven't been able to have a meter fitted at all. Instead, electricians have simply run a cable from a nearby property (sometimes even running it for a hundred metres across an olive grove) to theirs so that they can at least have mains power until things can be sorted out. The problem has been in so many cases that the householder had been left by a builder, who's all but vanished, with a "piggy-back" supply of electricity which is highly illegal, not to mention dangerous, and no way of knowing how to get the paperwork sorted out and get their own legal meter installed. One development of about twenty bungalows in a village not too far from us, where incidentally the 'builder' was a very crooked British man, left five houses running off of one meter. After several of these had been living like this for a year or two, the electricity company sent engineers to disconnect all of the 'piggybacking' houses, leaving them without power for an indefinite period. Remember in chapter 5, when I mentioned how familiar I am these days with portable electricity generators?

In the case of our build, we, or rather our landlords, got off fairly lightly. I say 'fairly' because at least we did get a meter installed after we'd been here for three months, on 'builder's supply'. This was because the builder had had a falling out with a couple of suppliers and thus couldn't show receipts for the tiles used in the build, the doors and windows or the wiring job done by the installing electrician. No receipts meant no domestic supply. It only took eight years, a huge amount of stress and a lot of expense for John to finally get it all sorted. That involved hiring a succession of lawyers and accountants, each of whom swore that they'd sort it out. After they'd demanded successive sums of cash and not produced results, he'd had to write them off as bad jobs and move on. The biggest problem was the fact that the builder, who was British, had moved back to the UK leaving not only our landlords, but several other people who'd bought houses that he'd built in the lurch. To be fair to the builder in question, he'd tried to display honesty and integrity. He had paid all the taxes on the build for example. He was, however, eventually beaten into submission by the whole system out here and was left with little alternative.

See? I said that this chapter would be one for the 'negative column', didn't I? To return to the fact that I placed the word builder/builders in parentheses, this is because there are, believe it or not, some reputable building companies out here doing a fairly good job. The problem largely was the boom in the noughties, which attracted all kinds of speculators who weren't really builders. Foreigners seeing ads in the Sunday papers were not to know just how awful things could be if they were to start a business relationship with a charlatan.

At the outset I mentioned Alf, whose house went up without too much fuss and, owing to the fact that he was here to keep a watchful eye on the proceedings, he was able to head off any problems before they got out of hand. So, if you want my advice, always assuming you might still be thinking about coming out here after all of the foregoing, here it is…

Well, actually, no. Hold on a moment. There's Brexit. That's kind of brought to a halt virtually all prospects of British people buying out here for many years to come. I don't doubt that most will be wanting to see exactly what relationship the UK eventually has with Greece when it comes to visas, health care, pension and tax issues and the like once the UK is no longer in the European Union.

It may surprise you though, that there are still ex-pats from the UK, Germany, Russia and a few other countries moving out here to live. What the majority are doing though, is finding somewhere to rent, rather than buying.

My advice? If you're at that stage in life where you're quite well set up, if your health is generally good, if you think you can manage without having to depend on working over here, then by all means come over and rent somewhere, even if just for a fixed period of time as a taster. That way you get the best of both worlds. If things go pear-shaped, you can leave with minimum fuss.

Despite all the stuff I've referred to in this chapter, day to day living out here can be very pleasurable. As long as you keep the right company, that is.

8. Social and Domestic

When you first get here you have no idea what to expect when it comes to your social life. You may think you do, but you don't really. It doesn't take long to start running into other ex-pats. You'll see them at the local supermarket checkout, when you wander into a coffee bar during the day time or a taverna or bar at night. The general impression one has is that there'll be all these folk acting very laid-back and enjoying life in the sun.

Everyone's background is, of course, different and mine involved a lot of Greek relatives, plus Greek company, even in the UK before moving out here, owing to my wife's Greek heritage. The fact that she could already understand the language and speak it haltingly led us perhaps in a different direction from many ex pats who arrive here and start looking for a social life. For reasons that there's no need to go into here too, we kind of had a ready-made group of Greek friends within a few days of our arrival, which was a great help.

It's important to remember that, once you get out here the shoe, if you like, is on the other foot. Back in the UK *we* were the indigenous ones, it was *our* country. Foreigners coming into the country could expect antipathy if, for example, they refused to integrate or learn the language. So often you'll hear a British person, while still at home in the UK, say "When in Rome…" when discussing the culture and conduct of immigrants living there. Sadly, when they get out here many forget this principle. One of the hottest potatoes in the UK nowadays is immigration. No doubt something that riles many is the tendency that immigrants into the UK have to develop "ghettos", areas where, but for the climate, you could be forgiven for thinking that you'd been whisked away to Pakistan or somewhere when you walk along a shopping street or around a housing estate. Such situations arouse strong feelings.

Living in Greece when you're born and raised somewhere else makes *you* the immigrant, the interloper, the one needing to remember whose country this is and yet it seems to me that quite a lot of ex-pats out here are insensitive to the facts.

The way the Greeks treat domestic animals, as an example, has many a UK ex-pat seething. First and foremost, since one has to be so careful these days as it seems to me that everyone's so quick to rise, I love animals and can't abide seeing them ill-treated. That's one reason why I don't eat them. That said, there is, it seems to me, a need for more balance. To love animals and to want to see them treated kindly is one thing, whereas to view a domestic pet as "one of the family" is different. There are many, and here I go getting all controversial, who treat animals as though they were humans. They are not. To demonstrate kindness to animals does not necessarily entail that one surrenders to sentimentality and, here goes, I do believe that a lot of us British are guilty of that.

Out here the culture, especially on the islands and in mainland rural communities, has for centuries involved people viewing animals as something to be employed, put to use. Even in the UK we use dogs as security, as the number of signs on gates declaring that there are guard dogs present indicates. Cats are used to keep vermin down. I used to live in a village near the South Wales coast and our regular country walks down to the beach took us past a fenced enclosure where plant and machinery was kept. Inside this enclosure was the most ill-tempered German Shepherd you could ever wish not to meet. If you got to within a metre of the chainlink it would throw itself at the other side and leave you certain in the knowledge that, were it not for that fence, you'd be minus your throat in seconds.

Admittedly it's probably more ubiquitous out here than in the UK, but it isn't as though in the UK we have the monopoly on animal welfare. Nothing gives us the right to land here and then begin campaigning about how cruelly the Greeks treat their animals. Some time back I was reading a Facebook post by someone who'd had their dog poisoned. I may not get the exact words, but the comment went something like:

"What am I doing living in this barbarous country?"

Frankly, I felt the same. What *were* <u>they</u> doing here? I started to think about badger baiting, hare coursing, rabbiting with small dogs or ferrets, fox and deer hunting on horseback with dogs, dog-fighting and cock-fighting, most of which still go on in the UK. The list of the indictments against UK society where animal cruelty is involved is sadly pretty impressive.

So, one has to ask, what right do we have to come here and then start railing against our hosts in such a manner? Generalisations are seldom a good idea. There are very many Greeks who are dedicated to animal welfare, plus many organisations, including one which sends vets out to the islands and rural areas on a regular basis to catch and neuter feral cats to try and contain the growth in their numbers.

Feral cats, now there's a subject. These animals are wild. They have been for generations. The trouble is, they look exactly like domestic cats and thus ex-pat Brits especially can't help themselves emitting an "oh, isn't he cute," when they see one. Well, to be honest you seldom see just the one. Where there's one there's usually half a dozen or more as I'm sure you don't need me to tell you. If they were much more ugly like, say, a rat, maybe more people would exhibit more objectivity. Instead what predominantly British folk living here have done is exacerbate the problem of feral cats beyond all recognition. They do this by feeding them.

In this part of Rhodes, for example, I know personally of several UK couples who buy dry cat food in those big paper sacks from the supermarket, then go out and do a tour of all the bins in the area sprinkling little piles of food for the feral cats to eat. Their motives aren't in question. But I would venture the suggestion that they may just be misguided.

I'll illustrate in a very graphic way. Some years back my wife and I stood on the North rim of the Grand Canyon in Arizona. We were reading a view-point sign and generally being awed (in the US everything's 'awesome' after all) when we detected a movement to our right. Turning, we saw a magnificent adult female deer approaching us, looking curious. She came within probably ten feet of us. Why did she do this? Where was her fear of humans?

Well, at the time we were both munching on sandwiches that we'd prepared as a picnic before we'd made the incredibly long drive to get there from our overnight hotel. It was then that our eyes were drawn to yet another sign, posted for visitors to read, which said something like, "Do NOT feed wild animals. As soon as you feed them they begin to see humans as a food source. This is the first step in them losing their natural habits as wild animals and thus more often than not the park rangers then have to shoot them."

Deer had been known to seriously injure people's hands, as once they'd been fed by a human they began assuming that every human hand held a tasty morsel for them. They aren't by nature aggressive, they simply want to eat.

What has this got to do with feral cats in Greece? Well, I see the parallel there in that if misguided, well-meaning foreigners hadn't started feeding feral cats in the way that they now do, these cats would not have started becoming domesticated. These animals are natural foragers and rodent-catchers. Their numbers were always regulated, before we soft Brits turned up, by their own success or failure in scavenging food. Now they are being fed by humans (and in Pefkos not far from here there is even a "cat feeding station" which sports some stainless steel dishes bolted to the top of a wall into which people can place cat food, and they do, believe me they do), their numbers are increasing alarmingly and the problem is getting worse, far worse. Their numbers increase because well-meaning foreigners, by feeding them, have increased their level of health and thus their ability to breed more successfully. Plus the newborns are seeing a much greater survival rate than they would if left to their own devices. In nature, it's survival of the fittest, misguided humans are changing that balance when it comes to the feral cat population.

You can add the dog situation to that problem too. Granted, here is where the average Greek living in rural areas and on the islands may be badly in need of education about the need to neuter their animals, but once again foreigners here, by their nurturing dogs and refusing to have the excess of newborn puppies "put down" humanely, have exacerbated the problem of the sheer number of dogs existing in areas like this. It's my feeling, although I greatly dislike cruelty, that the foreigners have contributed to a situation which, however distressing it may be, is tantamount to communities like the one we live in here on Rhodes becoming buried in a mountain of cats and dogs. Their numbers have multiplied so far out of all sensible proportions – even in the decade-plus that we have lived here – that the cat and dog shelters, run by dedicated and without doubt caring people, are unable to cope with the ever increasing numbers. There's hardly a house that's lived in by UK ex-pats (some German, Dutch and other nationalities too) that doesn't have three or four dogs and you still see strays walking the roadsides. Some homes literally have dogs and cats everywhere. It smacks of things being out of kilter. My wife and I were just discussing this and she referred to just three couples that we know, all expats from the UK, who between them have fifteen dogs.

It's a hard one and a subject that one can be sure will draw a lot of flack against me, but realism and truth were never all that popular, as discussed in chapter four.

In nature animals cull each other all the time, often without consideration for the pain caused to the victim. We as humans have it within our power to redress the balance of the human-to-dog/cat ratio, but it would take some hard decisions and no little expense. What does grate, coming back to the ex-pat community, is that if one decides to not have pets, one so often senses here an evidently judgmental attitude on the part of some who do keep them. It could be argued that many who support the "rights" of dogs and cats perhaps have human relationship issues and thus this makes them more prone to resort to their animals and to saying things like "a dog will never stab you in the back" and the like.

I once had reason to discuss the difference between faithfulness and loyalty, under an entirely different and educational context. It struck me as very interesting that if you look up the definition of these words you'll find they are very, very different from each other. Loyalty is defined basically as "unwavering attachment to a person or cause until the purpose of that attachment is fulfilled." Faithfulness, on the other hand basically means "dependability". In the light of this it is wholly wrong to conclude that a dog, for example, could be loyal. A dog can certainly be faithful, in the sense that inanimate objects also can be faithful. The moon, for example, can be described as 'faithful' because you can predict when it's going to rise, when it's going to set and what part of its phase it's going to be in at any time. It's dependable. A dog is like that to the extent that it will be reliable, it will do what you expect it to do in any number of given circumstances. Let me kidnap your dog though, let me give it choice doggy treats and a comfy bed to sleep in. Let me shower it with affection and you can be sure that its attachment to you will soon become a thing of the past. Were it ever to see you again, sure it would recognise you, no doubt be pleased to see you, but loyal? Nope, because it's not attached to you in the way a man or woman can be to their spouse, or their parents, even their country, dare I say their god.

Out here, especially during the winter months, there are often charity events to help the dog and cat rescue centres. This is good. This is right. My wife and I attend these whenever we can. Once one has an animal in one's charge it is only just that one discharges that responsibility in a way that nurtures that creature. These events often take the form of a coffee morning at a bar, or maybe a bring and buy sale. This gives me the opportunity to return to the subject of how the ex-pat community functions, or doesn't, as the case may be.

Since coming to live here in Rhodes we've made some good friends with some very nice people. What soon becomes apparent, though, is that many are of the mentality that dictates that they be in some way in competition with you. Who knows the most about how the system works, about the bureaucracy and how to get things done, about the Greeks and what they're like.

We hadn't been here too long when someone who'd already lived here for many years gave us a pep talk about why there's not much point in learning the language. This individual had no inkling at all of my wife's family heritage, of the fact that she had a Greek mother and had spent years immersed in Greek family, traditions and cultural mores. She just set to with a lecture about what we were to expect having now relocated to Rhodes.

"The Greeks don't like you learning Greek." She said.

"Why not?" We asked.

"Because they only want to speak English and they think you're only trying to ingratiate yourself if you attempt to talk to them in Greek".

She had much more advice besides.

"Never trust any of them. All the men are after sex and everyone worships money. They'll befriend you, but only until it's of no more use to them financially. They despise us and I find you need to keep an air of aloofness."

I could go on. It turned out that this individual has precious few friends and even less Greek ones. No surprises there then. Having got to know her, we both decided that she actually is very sweet and has a heart of gold. Her main problem is that she's wrong about so many things and isn't inclined to want to be adjusted in her opinions. Hey ho. The trouble is, there is a tiny grain of substance to what she said, but she exaggerated it out of all proportion. I'll give an example.

Some years ago we took a holiday on Crete with some very close relatives, another couple. We stayed in studios in a modestly sized block on a hill above the tiny resort of Makry Gialos in the South East of the island. There were probably eight studios and one apartment with a couple of bedrooms that had recently been renovated, plus a small pool. It was very intimate and located just a short walk of about a hundred metres up a path from the road. From the tiny balconies one had a spectacular view along the beautiful spoon-shaped bay, at the far end of which was the tiny harbour consisting of a pile of rocks forming a breakwater. It was just about perfect for me and the beloved. We knew, though, that we were taking a gamble going with this couple because they were the types who generally preferred posh hotels with room service, plenty of polished marble and potted plants. I'd tried almost to dissuade them from coming in an effort to stave of any complaints about the standard of the accommodation. I stressed again and again that it was modest, but essentially Greek. There'd be no room service, but in all likelihood there would be some nice interaction with the owners and other locals. All together it ought to have been an enriching experience.

The first day or two went OK. The place wasn't full, but there were several other studios that were occupied. Sitting around the pool we met another couple who were very personable, intelligent, articulate and the pair of them were like us, avid readers. And they were dedicated Grecophiles. They told us that it was their third or fourth time staying at these studios because they loved it there so much. What put the icing on the cake was the fact that the 'landlady', Despoina, who was about fifty with the usual dyed brown hair and a flowery-patterned sleeveless housecoat permanently adorning her person, would spend a few minutes each evening with her guests around the pool, always bringing with her some little morsel for her guests to sample.

We soon discovered what they meant. It was September, so it didn't get dark until about seven. We wouldn't go to the pool until four or five in the afternoon and then spend a few hours there. Shade was provided in the shape of several umbrellas, plus a pergola at the end of the pool terrace closest to the house. Under the pergola were some very comfy circular tables and chairs, the ideal place for an early evening gin and tonic. *Kyria* Despoina would appear from around the side of the building at around 6.00pm., always with a plate or a dish in her hands. She'd sit at one of the tables and show us what she'd brought for her guests to sample. One night it may be homemade bougatsa, halva or milopita, another it would be something savoury, like perhaps dolmades or courgette rissoles (*kolokithokeftedes*). She always made sure to bring enough for everyone and would frequently tell us that she didn't view her guests as paying visitors, but rather as family.

Kyria Despoina would sit and ask her guests all about their lives and families, plus she'd answer our questions about hers. She was a genuine person, trying to make a living by being good at what she did. We'd been there probably almost a week when our relatives began telling us about an awful smell coming from the drain in their ensuite shower room. We went up to investigate and offer an opinion and suggested that they talk to Despoina or her husband, who would surely do something to sort the problem out. I fail to see why they'd have wanted to do otherwise, because it would serve no commercial purpose whatsoever to have guests posting on Trip Advisor about smelly drains, or going home with horror stories which would dissuade others from coming to these rooms.

Basically, our relatives did a moonlight flit. First we knew was after they'd moved out. They'd asked about a room at an apartment complex down near the beach, where there was a huge pool and a ready-made gin and tonic brigade. It was a timeshare complex and many of those staying there were regulars, many with very red noses, and not from the sunshine. Our relatives had paid extra and taken a small apartment and were soon getting to know the UK brigade around the posh pool.

Meanwhile, Despoina, our landlady was inconsolable. We found her in a flood of tears fretting about what others would think of her if her guests felt that her accommodation was so bad that they had to move out. At the time we were there, the two-bedroomed apartment, recently renovated and very smart, was not occupied. Despoina pleaded with us to get our relatives to come back and she said they could occupy the apartment at no extra charge. It seems that they hadn't given her the chance to put the drain problem right by actually reporting it to her.

Of course the couple refused to come back and as far as I know never saw Despoina again. We were faced with the awkward situation of being on holiday with relatives who'd moved out and then wanted us to spend time around the pool at this very "British" apart-hotel, something which isn't our bag, pure and simple. Keeping our relationship going was a challenge in itself. Reluctantly we agreed one time to go down and sit by their pool and have a drink before going out for the evening. Signs around the bar area advertising karaoke nights, quiz nights and themed parties told us all we needed to know about the place.

The reason for telling you this story is the fact that the male of the couple to whom I'm referring, who is not a blood relative, was effusive in expressing his opinion that all Despoina wanted to do was take the money and run, to rip off her British residents pure and simple.

"She's only interested in your money, like they all are," was his view. He really had no knowledge of the Greek people, their cultural mores, their customs. He tarred all hoteliers and landlords/ladies the world over with the same brush. Had he a smidgin of knowledge about what the common or garden Greek is like he'd not have drawn the conclusions that he did. What upset us the most was the fact that they didn't a) report the drain problem to the owner to see if something would be done and b) they did a cowardly moonlight flit. I ask you, which is worse, being a negligent landlord or slipping away secretly in the night?

Suffice it to say that before one can make value judgements about others, one needs to have a solid foundation of knowledge. Which brings me back to the ex-pats living out here. I don't know, maybe it's just something in human nature, but we all seem to be so keen to offer advice don't we.

Take gathering firewood in the winter as an example. Lots of people here simply find out through the grapevine about a local who will sell them a truckload of logs for the fire for a 100 Euro or so. More than likely, the bloke who turns up at your front door with his load has been up in the forest and wielded his trusty chainsaw hither and thither in order to fulfil your order. He almost certainly won't be providing you with a printed receipt for the wood. But others, like us, like to find our own fuel for the woodburner.

The local municipality moves the goalposts from time to time it's true, but there are a few basics. Firstly, now and then they'll issue permits to anyone applying, allowing one to go and cut wood from dead and fire-burnt trees for their own personal use at home. This permit doesn't allow for commercial logging for re-sale of the wood. The reason is obvious, think how much a bloke with a chainsaw and a truck could strip out of the forest when it's for financial gain. There are, of course permits for the legitimate businesses who sell firewood, but to get one of these one has to be in business officially.

Nudge nudge, wink wink, eh?

Raise the subject in conversation with any number of swaggery expat Brits and you'll soon be undergoing a lecture about what you ought and ought not to be doing up in the woods. We're talking chainsaws here, just to be sure there are no misunderstandings. Every bloke you talk to about it will tell you something different.

"There aren't issuing permits this winter."

"You don't need a permit for gathering wood for personal use."

'The permits cost xxx Euros."

"The permits are issued for free."

The permit permutations are endless.

What really gets me down is the pettiness that so many display. I've probably written about this before, but the foreign communities in places like this are a cobbled together mishmash of folk who probably wouldn't be friends back in their home country. Moving out here you suddenly find that your social life is carried on among people with whom you have no history. All the people you've been close to for all of your life up until the moment when you left your homeland are now a long way away. You have to find someone new to go out for a drink or a meal with, to invite to your barbecue etc.

Very soon it becomes apparent that to immerse yourself in one of the enclaves, and these exist all over an island when it's the size of Rhodes, you'll soon be treading on thin ice with whatever company you are keeping. People seem to fall out with each other for a living. They take offence, occasionally also someone else's spouse or partner, they make up stuff about each other. Why? I dunno, to score points I suppose.

I do a few excursions for a part time job during the summer season. During the 2013 season, in July, my mother died and at the drop of a hat I had to fly back to the UK. I was the executor for her will too, so it meant our being away for at least some weeks. The day I left I telephoned the office of the tour operator for whom I was working and explained what had happened and the fact that I needed to go back to the UK immediately.

Elena, in the office told me, "No problem John. So sorry about your loss. The job's going to be here for you when you get back."

In actual fact I'd found someone who could fill in for me. So she fitted right into the excursion schedule and the company was happy.

A week or two after we finally flew back here to Rhodes and I'd resumed doing my job, we were sitting having a drink with a British friend in a nearby village. She told us, "Alan told everyone while you were away that you'd lost your job with [she named the tour operator]."

Alan was this person's next-door neighbour. He was also a kind of friend of mine. To be honest, I'm still friendly with him because I decided not to go and confront him about this little exaggeration that he'd allowed his imagination to fall victim to and then spread abroad. I'm not claiming to be the only sensible person out there, but others would probably have either had a blazing row with him or simply stopped talking to him, which is more often the case.

This is where the thin ice comes in. You can invite a few people for a get-together and you'll almost certainly be quizzed by some of them about who else is going to be there. It's like everyone's got their own list of acceptable and non-acceptable company and you have to know who's on each person's list or you'll find no one wants to come to your party.

I know, I make it sound so sordid. Hmm, well, there you are.

To try and redress the balance a little, there are some really nice, genuine people out here. There are some we'd count as having become true friends. You walk, though, a very fine line if you try to keep out of all the intrigues that go on.

When I was at junior school, I used to keep company with my few real mates in our own corner of the playground. There used to be the 'big boys' who'd think nothing of duffing you up if the opportunity presented itself. There'd be the ones you couldn't trust with a secret because you just knew it would be all around the school in minutes if you told them. There were the cry babies and the smelly kids. There were the gangs, all of which had their loudmouthed leader that the others all follow blindly. We've all been there.

In an ex-pat community, sadly, many think they still are.

9. Moving About

We all make plans. We had a plan about moving out here. We were going to get ourselves settled, then maybe go island hopping now and again. Of course, it never really happened. There are, though, a number of reasons for this, not all of them the obvious one, laziness.

You have to have a financial plan. We have come across people who've made the move and had to abandon their dream after a while and return to their homeland because they hadn't a good enough financial plan. The ideal situation to be in is to be rich. That's a surefire way of managing OK. Failing that, have at least enough financial backup to be able to deal with the occasional disaster. Don't come out here with children of school age. That would be my advice. They'll settle in, true, but unless you speak Greek you'll be no help to them at all when they have difficulty with their homework.

You'll be like a deaf mute at parent-teacher evenings. Frankly, whilst the level of education out here is by no means poor, it probably doesn't compare favourably with that of the UK, or many other Western European countries, or the USA.

To be honest (hot potato time again), religion is part of the reason. If you want your kids to grow up open-minded then the Greek system isn't the one to do it in. Religion still plays an inordinately large part in daily life and this also applies at school. In the villages the local *papas* still wields an uncomfortable amount of authority and reaches easily into the local school and its daily life. Children from religious minorities don't get an easy life at all, nor do their parents. The pressure to comply with all kinds of outdated customs and superstitions is immense. I know, more enemies in the making, but I don't subscribe to the view that all the icon-kissing and incense-waving stuff is harmless tradition or simply the culture. A little research shows that it's all based on falsehood and superstition. Basically, it enslaves people to irrational beliefs and fears. Religion really shouldn't be thrust in people's faces while they go about their daily secular lives. This applies in school especially, because children are impressionable.

Once you are here, moving about on a daily basis requires an adjustment in one's thinking, especially on the roads. You know, like, in the UK there are lines in the centre of the road and lines along the kerbs to tell you when you can or can't overtake, where you can and can't park, or at least what times of the day you can or can't park. By and large we all tend to take notice of these lines as we think it makes for an organised society, which to a degree it does.

Here, those lines are virtually invisible. By and large they follow the same rules as they do in Britain. For example, two unbroken lines in the centre of the road mean no overtaking. Actually, to be precise, if you read the British Highway Code it says that an unbroken line is not to be crossed, which usually means no overtaking, but there are rare situations where one can get past another vehicle without crossing the line and, if so, no law has been broken. One unbroken line and one dotted line means that vehicles on the side with the dotted one can overtake, whilst vehicles on the other side can't. This works well on some bends, where traffic coming one way can see a lot further around the bend than can drivers from the other direction. Yellow lines along kerbs in urban areas dictate the rules on parking in that area. One single yellow line and you can park on it during the off-peak overnight hours. Two unbroken yellow lines and you can't park there at all, ever. Unless of course you're a white van man, but then most of the rules of the road don't apply if that's the case (I know, cheap jibe, sorry!).

I said that the lines on the road here are invisible. This applies in two ways. The first is in the sense that no driver as far as I can tell ever takes the slightest notice of them. The second is the fact that the local authority here on Rhodes uses the cheapest paint it can get its hands on to apply the lines and thus they regularly wear away to either virtually invisible or completely obliterated within a few months of those chaps with the funny line painting machines having done their meticulous job. I wouldn't be surprised if those white lines weren't laid with basic interior grade emulsion paint, supermarket own-brand quality. On offer.

We hadn't been here even 48 hours when I began to get the measure of how to treat the road lines when driving, which basically means to completely ignore them, like they are invisible. If you want to pass a slower vehicle, what you do, in essence is this: You approach to within a gnat's whisker of the bumper of the vehicle in question, always assuming that it has one. You watch the traffic coming in the opposite direction for a gap barely large enough to allow you to make the pass and you shift down, whip out from behind him/her, trying to ensure that your nearside wing misses his tail light by a hair's breadth, then you cut back in just close enough to alarm him but not so close as to actually belt his front wing.

What you don't do is take any notice of what the lines are doing in the middle of the road. They're for decorative purposes only.

Going back to the point about the lines wearing away. A good example of how this makes for endless fun is the fact that in the past few years a few roundabouts have been installed on the "Rodo-Lindou" main road, ie. the road that runs the length of the East coast from Rhodes town to Lindos, much of which has been upgraded to a dual carriageway in recent years. The first roundabout one encounters making the trip from Rhodes Town to Lindos is at the last junction from which one can enter the village of Arhangelos. Now, here's the thing: In Greece generally they have a rule for junctions, especially roundabouts, and it's this: Give way to vehicles coming from your right. Quite a few junctions in Rhodes Town have those little concrete islands in the middle, the kind that a traffic policeman can stand in, whistle between his lips, as he leads the traffic a merry dance. Not that you often see one there, most of the time it's get on with it and keep diligent, keep on the alert. Even if you're already on the roundabout, if there's a road to your right and someone's whizzing along it in your direction, they'll be expecting you to stop and let them cut across in front of you.

With this in mind, who in their infinite wisdom decided that when they constructed the new roundabouts (which, to list them all, are at Arhangelos, Haraki, Massari and Kalathos) they'd change the priority so that anyone already on the roundabout has right of way, much as it always has been in the UK? It wasn't so bad when these were first opened for use. After all, the road paint was new and there were solid white bars across the road surface as you approached along with the word 'STOP', which seems to mean the same in any language of the world. As far as I could see, they've never erected warning signs a few metres before you get to the roundabout telling you who has priority. They've left that job entirely up to the paint that they applied to the road.

When the roundabouts were new, by and large people began to get the idea, with a few bodywork-crunching exceptions. Slowly, though, as the road paint has faded and it's no longer possible to make it out with any degree of clarity, we've arrived at the situation we have today, which is basically that as you approach a roundabout, you take your life into your hands. The one I most often have to negotiate is the one just outside of the village of Kalathos, near the Flevaris supermarket. I'm frequently coming down the hill from Pilona and the Lindos road is to my right. Assuming that no vehicles coming up from Kalathos want to proceed across my bow and go to Lindos, if I'm turning left toward Kalathos then I ought to be able to enter the roundabout and drive around it in safety.

It seldom works that way. If I'm the first vehicle to reach the roundabout, I can't simply proceed because nine times out of ten a banshee from hell will tear down the road from Lindos, to my right, and simply carry on regardless toward Kalathos. I've lost count of the times I've had to slam on the anchors to avoid being totalled by someone in this manner. On every occasion I've had the right of way. On every occasion that hasn't mattered one jot.

The scenario which really gets me going, though, is when I'm second or third in the queue and the vehicle in front entering the roundabout has seen that there is a vehicle coming from the right, but in this case both have stopped because neither is sure who has the right of way. The end result has so often been a stupid driver actually on the roundabout, stationary and waiting for the twit coming down from the Lindos direction to proceed, even though for some miraculous reason the twit has remembered who has right of way and who doesn't, and thus has also stopped. The absence of the lines, which have worn away to nothing, has resulted in a total free-for-all with one never being sure how other drivers are going to interpret the priority situation. The other side of this kind of scenario is when both keep going and either there's a near collision, or an actual coming together, bang, resulting in much horn blowing, window lowering and shouting and waving of hand gestures leaving no one in any doubt as to the physical act that the one gesticulating would like the object of their scorn to perform.

Approaching the roundabout at the bottom of the long hill running down to Arhangelos from the South one time, I saw a car cut up a huge tourist coach by zipping up the hard shoulder and almost causing the coach driver to hit him. The car had to skid to a halt at the last minute because the vehicle already on the roundabout which had right of way was a big dumper truck, something you don't argue with when your vehicle is a Citroen Saxo with go-faster alloys and an extra air-ram skirt on the front. The Saxo had squeezed back on to the carriageway right in front of the coach, whereupon, owing to the fact that the Saxo had to stop unexpectedly, the coach's driver leapt from the coach and ran to the driver's door of the Saxo with the intent of teaching the young tearaway a lesson which can't be taught from behind a desk.

The coach driver just had time to operate the door handle on the Saxo when the Saxo's driver, sensing that his next meal was very likely to have been prepared by the kitchen at the island's hospital, hit the accelerator and shot across the roundabout, door slightly ajar, and off up the road towards town with the greatest despatch. The coach driver strode back to his vehicle with a clear expression of disappointment on his face. Well, disappointment mingled with anger I suppose would be a better description. Fifty tourists narrowly escaped witnessing a duffing up of epic proportions.

Parking is something else one has to get used to. Rhodes town is an urban sprawl, OK a modest one by UK standards, but it has parking/traffic police and even parking areas where one has to pay and display. I steer well clear of those, I don't believe in such things. It's out in the villages where you can have the most fun. The largest village outside of the urban area of Rhodes Town is Arhangelos, which is twenty minutes up the road from where we live. There is a sufficiently interesting variety of shops there though to make a regular visit worthwhile, plus there is a disproportionately large number of coffee shops than you'd perhaps expect from a village of its size, so it's even more essential to go there from time to time.

Arhangelos is refreshingly 'untouristy', with a tiny amount of accommodation for tourists, much of which is outside the village itself anyway. It's a working village of largely rural folk, which means that if you sit at one of the coffee bars of a morning and watch the people driving by in cars, pickups or on motorcycles, most of the men will resemble a cro-magnon on a bad hair day. That's not to say that they're aggressive or unfriendly, they just look as if they've yet to discover the existence of razor blades well into their fifties. When you factor in the kind of thick, wavy hair a lot of Greek men are blessed with owing to heredity, you could be forgiven for thinking that there has been a mass break-out in a nearby mental facility.

What's odd is that, although the village is generally viewed as pretty rustic and unsophisticated, it still sports a generous number of chic-looking women with Mini Coopers and the like. Maybe Arhangelos girls like a bit of rough, which is not for me to say, of course. It's great, though, sitting in one of the coffee bars on the main street, seeing these long slender women in impossibly tight leather trousers and with their heads glued to an iPhone, strolling out of the nearby supermarket while a gorilla drives by with his pickup piled dangerously high with logs and an Alsatian dog with its head fully extended outside the passenger window.

The parking there is a treat. My wife continually gets herself all in a stressful tizz every time I drive through the village. She's always telling me to park on the edge of the village and "we can walk in". OK, so I do that quite often, but there are occasions when it's not the practical thing to do. And before you start with all this "you must be a chauvinist because you talk like it's always you behind the wheel" stuff, she drives the car more than I do percentage-wise, which is why I grab the wheel more often when we do go out at the same time.

There's an old Greek *Yiayia* friend of ours who lives in Lardos and she needs a prescription collected from one of the pharmacies in Arhangelos once a month. Why doesn't she use the pharmacy in Lardos? She's had a falling out with them. "Bunch of crooks in there" is her opinion. We're in no position to argue because we don't know the folk in there at all. Oh, actually, I tell a lie, because Panos works there in the evenings and he's a computer and internet whizz-kid who used to run his own business as a PC consultancy. He had to pack it in in the end because, although he was very busy with stuff like solving peoples' software problems, sorting out their internet connections and giving lessons on how to use Windows and the like, a pile of olive wood logs for his *soba* as payment for services rendered doesn't actually help him pay his tax bill. It can be tough trying to make a living legally in rural areas when most folk will either promise to pay you some time (but that usually means not in your lifetime) or they'll want to employ the barter system. You know, "How much do I owe you? Really, that much? OK, no sweat, you come eat in my taverna once a week for a month and we'll be quits, right?"

Returning to the delights of parking in Arhangelos, we occasionally collect our elderly friend's prescription, which can mean a flying visit at an hour when we don't want to stop for a spot of people-watching or to buy vegetables from the totally excellent fruit, veg and dried nuts kind of shop in the main street. There are few parking restrictions along most of the main street, which means that people can be very imaginative in the ways in which they leave their vehicles. There is certainly no lack of imagination on the part of the Arhangeleans. One time you can drive past and see all the cars parked a-la herringbone system, and another they'll all be parallel to the kerb. This is because someone will shoehorn their vehicle into a space even when it's patently obvious that there isn't enough length available. Once a couple of nearby vehicles have left the scene then others will follow the example of the one that's now left sticking out from the kerb at a forty-five degree angle and pull up next door at the same angle.

All that aside, it won't make a bat's eyeball of difference to those who always double park anyway. It's what the hazards are for isn't it? A least that's the way most locals around here seem to understand it. If you switch on your hazards (which, correct me if I'm wrong, are meant for cases of emergency, right?) then it allows you to do whatever you damn well want to with your vehicle. Leave it double parked, leave it triple parked, leave it sideways in the middle of the road, but as long as you've switched on your hazards, well, that's all right then. Thus the situation that usually prevails when we go there, double and triple parking is the norm and you could be forgiven for thinking that you're at a fairground there are that many flashing lights. OK, so they're all orange, but it still creates that jolly atmosphere.

I haven't even touched on the area of the moped, scooter or motorbike. If you're a seasoned visitor to Greece then you'll know all about that. It's no surprise that almost daily on the local newspaper's web page there are reports of deaths and injuries to two-wheeled travellers, many of whom still don't wear a helmet. Judging by the number of near-misses I've had with scooters whizzing up the inside or weaving along the queue at the traffic lights so that they can position themselves bang in front of your number plate and slightly over the well-faded white line while we all await the green light, I guess I'm pretty lucky not to have a few of such collisions under my belt by now.

Of course another aspect of people moving about in the past few years here has been the *prosfiges* [refugees] or *metanastes* [migrants]. It's a tough one and I'm in no position to proffer solutions to this mammoth problem created by man's inhumanity to his fellow man. I can, however, make a few observations. The most important angle on this whole distressing situation here is how it affects the tourist industry. Sounds shallow I know, but the Greek economy and especially the economy of the islands in the Eastern Aegean stands or falls on income from holidaymakers. In fact the influx, nay – at one point flood - of people arriving on some of the islands has affected places where it oughtn't even to be an issue, often because of misleading media reports, or simply as a result of people in northern Europe being ignorant of the geography of the area.

As an example, I've been told by someone who lives on the island of Poros, which is in the Saronic Gulf near to Pireaus and the Eastern Pelopponese, that she's been contacted by folk in the UK worrying about whether it would be safe to holiday there, owing to the refugee crisis, which is in fact taking place several hundred kilometres to the East from Poros and thus having no effect on the place at all.

Even on those islands that have borne the brunt of the influx, the situation is far from the way that it's been portrayed in the media. People in the UK (and I've been told by Dutch, Scandinavian and German tourists that it's the same in their countries too) have been given the impression that the entire island of, say Lesbos, is teeming with desperate people, that the beaches everywhere are covered in piles of discarded life-jackets and that there are issues with crime and unrest. Just a small amount of research, which nowadays is easily accomplished by using the internet, and one could readily discover that probably on 90% of that island it's been business as usual. Well, it would be if the tourists would come, but they aren't coming any more. Following the almost daily reports on the TV news in the UK during the 2015 season, the alarming and potentially devastating news at the start of the 2016 season was that tourism to Lesbos was virtually non-existent. Tour operators announced that planned flights to the island would be reduced by 80%. The consequences for taverna owners, hotel owners, shop owners, bar owners, excursion boat owners and all the employees in such places were catastrophic.

What is so annoying is the fact that so much of Lesbos was still looking as beautiful as it ever did, many of its beaches bore no evidence whatsoever of abandoned inflatables or discarded life-jackets.

We've all read the inspiring stories too of local folk who showed extraordinary kindness to many of the refugees. I have read stories of British holidaymakers who did stay in parts of the island where the refugees were much in evidence, who returned home feeling refreshed and rewarded after having been involved in the help operation.

What the eventual outcome of all this will be is not something any of us can predict. What I do know though is that the Greek government has done woefully little to help the local businesses on the islands that have been worst affected. They have actually made things worse by removing the VAT discount that the Aegean islands used to enjoy over the mainland. This special rate had enabled the islands to keep prices down for everything that has a connection to tourism. There have been massive hikes in VAT countrywide under the Syriza Government anyway, but when you add to this the removal of the discounted VAT rate that the islands used to enjoy, you realise that they've had to cut their profit margins to the bone rather than increase prices to such an extent that it would put people off coming again.

For a couple of decades and more there has been a steady trickle of immigrant workers coming into Greece from other Balkan nations. These are the ones who have come here not as refugees, but as economic migrants. Probably the majority of these are from Albania.

When we first arrived I, like most people, probably didn't have any idea of the numbers of Albanians that live even in the remotest of villages. There are a few other ethnic minorities here too of course, notably Bulgarians, but none can match the numbers of the Albanians. To get some idea of what's happened since the fall of the communist regime under dictator Enver Hoxha, the population of Albania is only something approaching three million. Between 1991 and 2004, some 900,000 people emigrated from the country for economic reasons and, of these, 600,000 have come here to Greece. That's a sizeable chunk of the Albanian people. And they're still coming.

Although on "paper" it seems as though Albania is a progressive country (for example, it as a health care system that attempts to care for every citizen without cost, although in recent years this has come under increased strain to the point where if you need treatment, invariably you have to pay for it privately), the economy is in dire straits, thus the mass exodus.

When I would go into a village square here before I really began to learn Greek, I would see men gathered around in knots, or perhaps sitting in the kafeneion smoking and making a Greek coffee last a very long time, usually during the morning hours from 8.30am until midday. By and large these were hanging around waiting for someone, perhaps a builder, to come along and offer them a day's work for cash in the hand. As the years progressed I began to understand better, as I could identify spoken Greek, that by far the majority of these men were Albanians. The frequency with which you see the "available for work" crowd has declined since the austerity kicked in of course, as the government tries to crack down on illegal employment. Ostensibly this is meant to protect workers' rights, but in reality it's brought more difficulty to many of these men who have families to support and probably are here illegally and have no papers that would allow them to work legally.

It's a tough one. Many Albanians have gone through the process of legalising their residency here in Greece, but a huge number are still here illegally. Fuel for the flames of "*hrysi avgi*", or Golden Dawn, the very right wing neo-fascist party that's begun to rear its alarming head in the past few years. It's strange, because if you read the manifesto of Golden Dawn, a lot of it looks on the surface to be fair and just.

The problem lies primarily with the way the party's supporters and indeed senior members conduct themselves. From 2011 through 2014 there were successive physical attacks on foreigners, including black-clad mobs with clubs destroying street vendors' stalls that they deemed illegal or as staffed by foreigners who ought to be kicked out of the country. On national television in June 2012 during a talk show, prominent Golden Dawn spokesman Ilias Kasidiaris assaulted a female MP live on the air with his fists after she'd allegedly thrown a newspaper at him during a commercial break. He was subsequently locked in a room at the TV studio, presumably while they decided what to do with him, since he was behaving violently, but he broke down the door and left the building. This man has large swastikas tattooed on both shoulders. More recently it appears that the party's support has begun to wane somewhat, but at the time of writing they still have a number of MPs sitting in the Greek parliament, including Mr. Kasidiaris.

In fact, I had a passing acquaintance with a British man who was living entirely legally in Athens a few years ago. The only problem is, he was of Asian descent and clearly looked it. He was advised to move back to the UK owing to the risk to his personal safety on the streets of Athens having become an issue.

Over the years that we've lived here on Rhodes we've become friends with a lot of Albanians. By and large they come across to us as hardworking, friendly, well-mannered and they keep their homes spotless. Right now we have some friends who live not far from us who are living in rented accommodation (which of course the vast majority do) that in the UK would be condemned as unfit for human habitation. I cannot begin to describe all the problems that they have with the property they live in, yet still the wife cleans and mops, the husband tries to decorate and they are always clean and "well turned out", as we'd say in the UK. They have a young child of school age and a new baby. The school age child of course is Greek in every way apart from the fact that his parents are immigrants. He prefers to speak in Greek than Albanian, as is the case with all the Albanian children at school here in Greece. If you ask them why their landlord doesn't fix the leaky roof, the sink that's hanging off the wall in the bathroom, the dangerous ceiling light fittings and the broken wall sockets, why he doesn't do something about the damp in winter and the ridiculously strong drafts that blow through the place on cold, blowy winter days and nights, they'll reply that he'd prefer they move out if they're going to give him any grief.

I've lost count of the number of tenants we've known who've spent serious money fixing up dilapidated accommodation, only to then be given notice to quit by a delighted landlord who now feels he can repossess a renovated property and do something else with it, like give it to someone in his own family for instance.

There are families here where the wife has all her papers and the husband doesn't. It's extremely complicated for some Albanians to get legal even if they want to. You'd assume that if one spouse in a marriage lives here lawfully, then it ought to be fairly straightforward for their spouse to get his or her papers sorted out. Frequently however, this is not so.

It's understandable why some Greeks resent the Albanians, but the issue is self-made. Plenty of those in the know will tell you that twenty years ago, when tourism was booming and Greeks ran businesses that made good money, they were very glad to have immigrants on hand to do all the menial jobs while the locals sat in kafeneions and played backgammon to their heart's content. Now, with the austerity hitting hard and employment having become a hot potato, suddenly the Albanians are resented for "taking Greek jobs". OK, this may be over-simplifying things, but, well, frankly it isn't.

What's quite distressing too is the way in which a lot of Greek employers talk to their Albanian employees. I've witnesses it first hand. Some bosses can't talk to an Albanian worker without it being in the form of a shout, or a barked order that demands instant response from the abused worker. Now, I wouldn't want to tar all Greek business owners with the same brush. I'm pleased to say that many are courteous and fair, but for every one who's like that there is someone who's of the other kind, sadly.

I think what perhaps also gets a Greek's goat is the fact the Albanians filter money out of the country. Quite a few of our Albanian friends are regularly asked by their family members back in Albania to send money for medical treatment. Without it the sick person would be in a very serious dilemma. Albanians are as a matter of course frequently bankrolling their families at home while also trying to make ends meet here. Thus a significant percentage of what they earn isn't plowed back into the local economy, but sent abroad.

Small wonder there appears to be a Western Union office in almost every village. This, though rankles with many Greeks. The British, by and large, do the opposite, earning money as they do from for example their UK pensions, they bring it over here to spend and thus inject cash into the Greek economy.

I do, though, when all is said and done, feel deeply for the dilemma that so many Albanians are in. The family I referred to earlier, whose home is barely fit for human habitation, have a lovely detached house back in Albania in their home village. It has an orchard and a garden all around the house itself. It is furnished and has a cosy log-burner in the lounge, but they can't afford to live in it. Virtually every Albanian couple I know owns property back home. Yet they live in substandard hovels in Greece because back home there is no means of earning an income. I was told just this week that if someone earns the equivalent of fifty Euros per month where they come from, they're doing well. Small wonder that many who still live at home in Albania subsist on home-grown vegetables and meat, plus the cash that their relatives in Greece send back every month.

Once again, it's a difficult dilemma. Who's to blame? It's unjust for the Albanians here to suffer persecution, yet many do and stoically live with it. They have little alternative. On the TV and in the newspapers, if there's a crime, the assumption is often made that it must have been committed by Albanians. In my experience of them, I find them often more likeable than many Greeks, and I love the Greeks – in general. How I would feel if I had to live over here in a hovel whilst back home I had a very nice property all locked up with a chain on the garden gate awaiting the possible future day when I may be able to come home to live in it once again, I really don't know.

I don't believe that I'd be smiling anything like as often as do many of my Albanian friends.

10. People

Generally I'm of the opinion that people are essentially the same the world over. They are, however, moulded very much by their country's culture and religion, even by their geographical location. The thing is, such things can make a huge difference.

One is reminded very often of the differences in what were for me at first unexpected ways. Then I got just used to them. I don't always like them though. I like to think of myself as a very logical person. I believe in true science, for example. Science has been defined as "the intellectual and practical activity encompassing the systematic study of the structure and behaviour of the physical and natural world through observation and experiment." Basically, what your observations and sometimes experiments reveal is what the honest, humble and true scientist should believe. Maybe in the future, with continued observation, some previous conclusions may be revised and changed. But basically, let the facts before you direct you to the most logical conclusion; to do that is to be a true scientist.

Which is why so many atheistic evolutionists are actually religious zealots. They already have their preconceived set of beliefs and refuse to acknowledge what the overwhelming body of evidence tells them, that there is design in nature. Don't worry, this isn't getting religious, you'll see where I'm going in a bit, honest. It would often amuse me if it didn't downright irritate to hear "scientists" accusing theists of precisely the same thing. Weirdly, in the majority of cases, I agree because there are so many people of various religious persuasions who believe such illogical things, who are willing to believe in absurdities because, well, frankly, because it's what they want to believe. But that's no excuse for so-called "scientists" to fly in the face of logic in that knee-jerk way that they do. Ie: because most religions preach rubbish, there can be no God. Babies and bathwater folks, babies and bathwater.

I like to think I walk the middle ground. Evidence presented before me by the universe and the natural creation observable here on our planet leaves me in no doubt that there is design and where there is design there is a mind. As a humble observer, who started out with no preconceived ideas at all (well, I was brainwashed with evolutionary thinking while at Grammar school), that's where logic takes me. Trouble is, start talking that way and those irreligious "scientists" jerk that old knee up immediately and shout "zealot! Simpleton!" But let's get one thing straight here – logical conclusions about creation do not send me running off to the nearest church. Far from it. Very, very far from it.

Not much I can do about those knee-jerkers, so I'll leave them to it. On the other side of the coin are all these absurd religions that pepper our planet and its cultures that frankly leave me amazed about how subjective the majority of humans are. That they're willing to be "preached into the trenches" by religions that seem to think that the almighty is of their particular nationality when there is a war is a prime and frankly terrible example.

Which brings me to the Orthodox church. There are, I'm relieved to say, plenty of modern intelligent Greeks who question much of what their "National" religion would have them believe. Their primary problem is, they're loath to stand up and be counted because the zealots (who are largely ageing nowadays as secularism is creeping in slowly, albeit about half a century after it did in the UK) will have their guts for garters if they don't go along with all the traditions, most of which are simply emotional and intellectual bondage to absurdities.

I often talk on the subject with Greeks in my neighbourhood, although, as is the case in the UK, a lot of men prefer to leave such matters to the women. But, boy, can a Greek woman of a certain age get hot under the collar about some things. So here I return to my comment earlier about how often I'm reminded of the cultural differences between here and the UK. I don't exaggerate when I say that I fully believe that much of Greek society is brainwashed by the Orthodox church. You could prove to someone irrevocably for instance that the church is entirely at odds with what the Bible says, but so many people will simply start slinging the mud of accusation that you must be in the wrong because everyone knows that the only true church is the Orthodox church and that's the end of the matter. Research, education, learning, these things matter not one jot to many such folk, who in all other areas of life may be quite kind, considerate and helpful. Oddly enough, some years back when we spent some time in County Cork, Ireland, the Catholics there were strikingly similar. Small wonder the atheists and humanists are gaining ground.

The UK is a largely secular society these days. I'm not saying that's necessarily a good thing but, if I'm honest, I'll say give me secularism over blind acceptance any day of the week.

Me and the better half, despite now having lived here for eleven years and counting, speak pretty good Greek. Yet, we still make it a point during the winter months when it's cold and dark outside to watch all the TV quiz shows going. We do this because it's an effective way of improving one's vocabulary. It's cheaper than lessons too. I don't exaggerate when I say that if you watch a cookery show, you'll see a chef, whether it be a woman or a man, cross themselves before sliding a dish into the oven to cook. They'll just as likely cross the dish too. If someone wants to win the jackpot on a game show, they'll think nothing of crossing themselves three or four times, all the while gazing upward in the vain hope that the almighty (or one of his representatives) may be more concerned with that person going home with a couple of thousand Euros than he is with a hundred and fifty refugees clinging on to a steadily sinking inflatable on a stormy, dark and cold Aegean Sea.

There's no getting away from it, to cross one's self is in essence a superstition. It has no basis at all in scripture and no logical reason behind it, yet the common folk of the Greek Orthodox church are compelled, I'd have to say by fear, to do it at every supposedly appropriate moment.

I work with quite a few coach drivers during the summer season, taking our guests on excursions. Some of the drivers I work with are now good friends. They'll carry on an animated and seemingly intelligent conversation with me about all kinds of subjects as we trundle around the island. Yet will they drive past a church or roadside shrine without crossing themselves three times? No way.

There are some reading this that would argue that there's no harm in it. 'So what if someone wants to do such things,' they'll say. 'Each to his or her own.' I'd have to question that point of view. It's the same church that indoctrinates folk to do such things that also gets them to believe that icons need kissing on certain dates each year, that a candle lit and placed in a holder inside a church will really make the difference for some loved one's prospects of survival as they lay in a hospital bed. The same church that, were Greece to go to war, would be very quick to encourage their youth to enlist and go off to fight. Yup, God is Greek folks. The thing is, he's apparently British, German, American and Iranian etc. too. He must be so confused.

Logic tells me that the almighty is far above such human rivalries. Logic tells me that I'm not more important when I send up a prayer for a big cash win (not that I would of course) in the national lottery than some poor unfortunate living in a doorway in Athens.

Yea, I know. I've gone on a bit about all this stuff. Sorry, but were Star Trek's Mr. Spock beside me I know whose side he'd be on. I got started on this purely from gazing at the sheer number of people who cross themselves every night on my TV screen and thinking how different this is from the common folk in the UK.

Turning to more positive, or at least more mildly amusing things, there are other aspects of society here that are much nicer than the UK. I was brought up in a village in England's West Country for most of my childhood. Back then our kitchen door was opened and closed with a simple metal latch, or lever. The idea of having to actually lock it was never heard of. Things have changed in the last few decades and changed beyond all recognition.

Here there are changes taking place too of course. In urban areas the catch-up with British and American society and all its ills is moving at a much faster pace than it is in rural communities. In Greek urban areas today security is becoming big business. Graffiti is everywhere and the TV news carries more and more reports of old folk being assaulted and robbed in their own homes. It's maybe because things are getting worse so fast that it's almost rippling through society like a shock wave. It took the UK most of my adult life to get as bad as it's getting in probably just one decade in Greece. I blame the media, especially American and British TV and movies. Sadly it's the case today that people derive their cultural mores from watching CSI or Bruce Willis. Every evening on Greek TV now after 9.00pm the majority of programmes are subtitled American crime dramas or foulmouthed and violent, often sexually explicit movies.

In the rural communities, however, there is still a marked difference in security matters between Greece and the UK. I have to say though, that over a decade on Rhodes has seen momentous changes for the worse. It's still true that cafés and bars leave their tables and chairs outside night after night with no fear of vandalism or theft. One could still leave one's car unlocked in most rural areas without any worries about someone either stealing the vehicle or something from inside it. You can walk the streets or lanes in relative safety without fear of assault.

Yet this is beginning to change for the worse. Many put it down to the severe economic crisis, the sheer number of immigrants, even tourists. But still when we arrived here in the summer of 2005, we spent a few years leaving all the windows open in the house while we drove to town for the day. That was during the time when we had no perimeter fence too. These days we tend to keep the garden gates locked all the time and never leave even one window open when we go out. Back in the beginning I never once locked my car, even when leaving it in town. These days I tend to lock it much more frequently, although not always, thank goodness.

When I was a boy, neighbours would drop in as and when they felt like it.

They'd still probably have knocked first though. Here, in country villages it's still like that, except the neighbours often don't feel the need to knock. Maybe it's born of the fact that many villages were almost entirely composed of extended families. It's still true to a large extent. Friends of ours in a village just up the road from us were talking to us just recently and the conversation went something like this:

"Do you know Maria is Manoli's daughter, Popi?"

"Yes, of course. Manolis is my first cousin. His wife Anoula is my second cousin. Nikolas who runs the bakery is my uncle and he married another of my dad's second cousins. You know that Litsa, who's marrying Savvas next month, is my niece too, don't you?"

"No, I didn't know that. Where's Savvas' family from, then?"

"Next village along. His dad is a relative of my mum…"

…and so on. Thus, they feel no need to shout a warning if they're wanting to see how you've rearranged the furniture in your lounge because, after all, they're family anyway.

Returning to the TV for a moment. I remember as a kid watching Pathé news, remember that? If you went to the cinema there would always be a B movies and a Pathé News bulletin as part of the programme. You got much better value for money at the cinema in the 50's an 60's than you do now. Since the demise of Pathé News though, it's doubtful that any serious news bulletin in the UK, especially on the TV, has had its voiceover accompanied by stirring, usually dramatic orchestral music.

Here it still happens. Every night on the TV news, regardless of which channel you're watching, they always feel the need to play some appropriate music behind the video reports. There may be a terrorist attack somewhere, perhaps resulting in a dozen deaths, yet Greek TV news will report on it with some dramatic music pounding out while they pull survivors from the rubble after the bomb or something. It's truly odd because it sort of trivialises the story and makes it as though it were a spoof or an excerpt from a movie and not as it really is, a traumatic event. You have to try and zone it out in order to take the report more seriously.

I still get asked regularly if I prefer living here to living back in the UK. It's an odd question really because here I am, here we are, after eleven years, still here. Yet we'd be far from truthful to answer simply that we prefer it here because everything's better. Everything isn't better. It's like moving house within your own country really though, even simply moving streets. When you move there are things about your new home that you're going to love and things about your old one you'll probably miss. The whole thing's always a matter of weighing the positives and negatives. On balance, we like living here enough to not hanker after going back.

Whether we'll still feel this way in a year, in five years, who knows? I'm not making predictions. Tell you what though, there are far worse places to live than this.

I'd say not many are better though. Not in today's world.

Just this past couple of days as I write this chapter in January 2017, we've remarked on how open and talkative, even cheerful most people are. I am British, I ought to spring to the defence of my fellow countryfolk, yet by and large I have to say that most people you encounter (not all, of course) are glum and look as though they've just lost £10 and found a fiver. I'll illustrate.

My wife was in the bank in Rhodes town on Monday. As ever, there was a long queue along the roped area while people waited to be served. Without warning the woman in front of my wife turned around and looked straight at her. This woman wanted to chat. They were soon talking about all kinds of stuff and the woman told my wife something interesting, if somewhat sad. She said, after my wife told her that she was half-Greek and that her mother had been from Athens,

"I knew you weren't English, at least not completely English. You smile. The English hardly ever smile."

You do have to get used to the fact that most Greeks have no concept of Britain and the countries Scotland, Ireland and Wales. If you're from those islands you'll be called an *Angle'zos* and you're from *Angli'a*. I've given up trying to explain that we lived in Wales before moving out here. I used to say "We had a friend in Wales who…" but became so used to being interrupted with "France? You had a friend in France?" This is because France in Greek is pronounced *Galli'a*, with a very soft 'g' at the beginning, and Wales is pronounced *Wali'a*. Since they're almost unconscious of the existence of Wales as a country, I used to begin explaining about where Wales is and yet nothing ever changed. So now I just accept it stoically. The Greeks, by and large, don't play rugby.

This very morning we dropped into the local "supermarket" along the road, the owners of which are Basilis ("Billy" to the UK ex-pats living here) and his wife Litsa. They are like the Greek Arkwright, the character played by Ronnie Barker in the classic UK sit-com "Open All Hours". Apart from very, very late at night, go past that store and it'll be open. Bank holidays? Open. Sundays? Open. There's even a caravan, the modest type that sleeps maybe three or four and can be towed by a family saloon, stationed just across the other side of the road where I'm fairly sure Basilis spends the night to save driving home to Asklipio village when he shuts up shop very late in the evening. That way he's ready to open his shutters at the crack of dawn.

So, there we were standing at the vegetables section when a Greek fellow of about forty struck up a conversation with us. He asked us how our winter was going and to remind him of where we lived. After we'd responded and joked about wishing each other *kalo mina* and the like… Hang on, let me start again, I wished him *kalo himona* (good winter) before realising that it was now well along and we're approaching spring already. He responded by saying, "Best change that to *kalo kalokairi!*" and beamed an infectious smile at us, then asked us how our winter was going and had we been back to the UK at all. After a few more comments were exchanged, he must have realised that we weren't too sure who he was, so he said "I'm from Lahania, my dad's the priest there."

"Ah, right! Giorgos, the good guy. Just about the only priest we get along well with." I replied, "He has the taverna…"

"That's right. Chrissie's."

And so it went on. We talked about the conversations we'd had with his jovial dad and asked if they were open during the winter months, to which he replied that they were, on weekends. We promised that one of these days we might drop in for a spot of lunch and another British couple who we'd been talking to chipped in that they'd bought potatoes from him in the past. Nothing spectacular, yet just an example of what regularly happens when you go shopping. When we reached Vasili at the cash register we again became immersed in a conversation with both he, his wife and two other Greek men who we didn't know at all. No matter, because we were soon nattering like old friends.

Of course such things happen elsewhere, but it's a symptom of the general sunniness of the Greek disposition that I'm trying to illustrate here. So rarely do such conversations turn to the negatives, so regularly they involve huge smiles and handshakes. I just seem to remember such occasions in the UK, when they did occur, being much "darker' in general. They would revolve around how awful the weather had been or how stupid this, that or the other politician was or how the prices had gone up so much lately that we'd soon be all begging on the streets. These folk that we live among here, they're suffering big time under the current economic situation. They have every reason to gripe and groan and yet more often than not they'll cheer you up.

I'm not trying to brag here, but I have to say that frequently such experiences happen because we speak to the locals in Greek. I've said it before and I'll repeat it here: Ex-pats ought to seriously consider why they aren't making efforts to learn the language. When the shoe was on the other foot and we were still in the UK, by far the majority of folk who now live as ex-pats out here would have been perched on a pub bar-stool ranting about how the ruddy foreigners who 'come over here' ought to learn to speak the Queen's English. 'When in Rome…' they'll have said. Now they live in Greece they're conspicuous by their silence on such an issue. They'll excuse themselves perpetually with the old chestnut "They all talk back to you in English."

Enough said. I've been there before.

It didn't take long for us to begin making friends and acquaintances once we'd begun our regular lives out here. Among the folk we've become quite close to are some who've been mentioned in the *"Ramblings From Rhodes'* books.

There's Mihalis, the smallholder with a house surrounded by a garden chock full of fruit trees and vegetables. His menagerie includes chickens, ducks, geese, rabbits and the odd dog or two. The latter of course are continually chained up near their kennels. I'll give him that, he does provide his dogs with kennels. Never seen him take either of them for walks though. At least they're well fed and watered.

Mihalis it was who used to leave plastic bags hanging from the car wing mirror with no fanfare. We'd arrive back at the car and find a load of lettuce seedlings in the bottom, or perhaps at other times of the year a few ripe, plump, shiny aubergines or courgettes. During the summer season we see him once or twice a week and he always has a tray of eggs for us. We'd never dream of refusing anything because it may send him the wrong signal that perhaps we don't want his gifts. We'll simply pass them on to other friends or our immediate neighbours if we have a too much of a surplus.

He's always ready with some advice about what particular day we need to be putting the beans in or what kind of *kopria* (compost) we need to put on which plants. He tells me when to thin out the beetroot and how to select which French bean plants to pull out and which ones to leave in to continue growing. He's generous with his produce and his counsel, yet incapable of commending me for whatever I do, even though I try hard to follow his advice.

We planted a new young orange tree a couple of years back. It's the navel variety that lots of people here favour, because it's a wonderful eater with the perfect balance between sweet and bitter taste and doesn't produce many pips. I planted it when Mihalis told me to and bought a very expensive liquid fertilizer on his recommendation. A one litre tin cost around 20 Euros, but you do dilute it quite a lot with water. I applied it as per his instructions and so, when he dropped by one day, I led him to the tree and showed it to him.

"Oh, I wouldn't have put it there." He said, then proceeded to point out everything that I'd apparently done wrong regarding location, light, soil and my dubious prospects of actually seeing a harvest of oranges any time soon. Some time later, in the spring, the young tree was absolutely covered in sweet-smelling white blossoms with delicate little yellow patches in the centre of each flower. I excitedly took a photo and showed it to him. I don't know why, I ought to have known him well enough, but I kind of expected him to say, 'Wow. How lovely. You'll be eating juicy oranges later in the year to be sure.'

Instead he took one look at the photo and said,

"That tree is sick, Gianni." and proceeded to offer more advice about how I might be able to save it from dying if I acted with enough despatch. I hadn't really noticed that the foliage had begun turning yellow. I thought that with all those blossoms on it, then it had to be happy and that we were indeed going to see a bumper harvest.

It seems that we'd done a very wrong thing. It was spring time and the rains were infrequent. We were watering the tree regularly as it was still only four feet high and we thought that it would need it, especially before the hot dry summer months came upon us.

"Oh, no, no. You should never water an orange tree when it's in blossom, Gianni." He told me. Dammit but it wasn't something we'd specifically covered during all our conversations up until then. He said that we only had to watch and all those lovely blossoms would drop off. Most of the leaves too.

They only went and did just that, didn't they. More recently we've talked with a few others about watering orange trees when they're in blossom and, sure enough, they all say the same. I don't pretend to understand it, but it must be right. At least the tree is still alive and this spring I'm flaming well not going near it with a hose pipe or watering can if it produces any flowers.

Some years back we used to quite often give a diminutive Bulgarian woman called Dopi a lift into town and back. In appreciation for our kindness she'd supply us with plastic bags full to bursting with wonderfully juicy oranges all through the winter months. This was due to the fact that she was a live-in carer, looking after an old *Yiayia* for a Greek family who had a business in Lindos and thus didn't have time to care for their old mum, who was slowly losing her marbles. The small cottage in which the two women lived was surrounded by a dozen orange trees, the fruit from which the woman's family would never bother to harvest. Thus, each time Dopi got into our car she'd emerge from the garden gate, vigorously 'shhhh-ing" me in a furtive manner and dashing up and down the path with three or four bags of oranges, which she'd bid me stow in the boot pretty sharpish. It was all a bit clandestine because the woman's children, all grown up and running their business, although they never bothered wth the oranges themselves, used to threaten her if she picked the fruit. It would sorely distress Dopi, well, us too, to see all these wonderful oranges being left to rot. So Dopi would go out and rattle the branches until the fruit dropped, then she'd gather up the fallers (seconds after they'd done so) and bag them up for us.

She'd get into the car saying, "Whenever they ask me, 'Have you been picking those oranges?' I can truthfully reply, 'no, I only gather up the fallers', tee hee."

Sadly, a few years ago our tiny, bow-legged, sixty-something Bulgarian friend with the shock of frizzy white hair returned to her native Bulgaria and we found our primary source of ripe oranges cut off. What on earth were we to do? To actually pay for our supply of winter oranges would be a painful experience.

Well, would you believe it but we became acquainted with a new family of Greeks from a village just up the road, and they have about fifty orange trees just outside the village of Massari. For the past six weeks or so, every time we see them, which is at least once a week, they're carrying plastic bags full-to-bursting with delicious navel oranges and those bags are destined for our car's boot.

So, here we are once again eating our morning muesli topped with chopped chunks of juicy, sweet oranges straight from the tree. Our fridge is stacked with small plastic water bottles whose use has now been turned over to holding freshly-squeezed orange juice and we're occasionally hanging bags of oranges on our neighbours' and friends' fences and gates to share the bounty with them too. There's an identical ongoing situation with lemons as well.

It's the same in June with apricots, in the high summer months with water melons. In May you can't move for cherries and in September watch out for those peaches, because it's easy to eat so many that you might just be well advised to carry some loo roll with you if you attempt a country walk.

In the UK you can waltz along the supermarket aisle and load up your trolley with whatever fruit you want, you pay no mind to what season the fruit's supposed to be grown in. It's shipped half-way around the planet to make sure that the supermarket shopper can have his or her choice of whatever fruit or veg he or she wants - any time of the year. Here one gets into the habit of buying local. It's not only a great deal cheaper, but it's far better for the environment and the fruit and veg tastes infinitely better for having been grown just along the road. The only slight drawback is, by the time you get to March/April, you feel like you never want to see an orange or a lemon again. You feel like you've almost turned into one or the other. It's OK though, because come November, you'll be eager to taste the first ripe oranges of the new season all over again.

Agapitos is another neighbour we've become well acquainted with. He's a sage old Greek with an allotment near our home. Here there is one of those rather unsightly concrete water cisterns perched on the crest of a hill, placed there to supply the tap water to the homes dotted along the coast road in Kiotari. Surrounding the cistern is a large fenced-off area, which is land belonging to Agapitos. Within this compound he's installed a pen for a number of dogs, another for his poultry, which also has a mesh roof on it to prevent predators like foxes from getting into or over the fence to dine on his feathered treasures I'd guess. Maybe the buzzards and golden eagles around here were eyeing the chickens, ducks, turkeys and whatever else he has in there with relish too, I don't know. Perhaps it was more a case of the birds getting out than a predator getting in. Whatever the case, he's built a 'soft' roof over it to make sure his supply of white meat or eggs is preserved intact.

He also has a large vegetable patch in there, plus a fairly useful olive grove consisting of a few older trees and about 30 young ones that he only planted a couple or three years ago. I call him "sage" with good reason. He hadn't long put the new olive trees in when we passed by during the early winter months to see him busily harvesting olives from these modestly-sized trees. They were still no taller than I am, yet they were laden with fruit. I suppose the fact that his allotment surrounds the water cistern may well account for the theory which I hold that he has an inexhaustible supply of water at his disposal, which I doubt he actually has to pay for. Whatever else he did to nurture those trees was certainly working, judging by the abundance of his first harvest.

He keeps a few dogs in a smaller compound, probably ten feet square and enclosed with rigid metal mesh fencing. His dogs, though, are well cared for. Agapitos comes to his allotment at least every day and often takes his dogs out for a walk. At the very least he lets them out of their pen while he works and gives them the run of the place. They have a couple of sturdy plywood kennels in which to shelter from either the hot sun in the summer or the driving rains during the winter and they always bark enthusiastically and wag their tails at us when we walk by. If we do so when Agapitos isn't there (the pen is probably thirty meters away from the perimeter fence and so we aren't able to get very close to the dogs), there is one of them in particular that amuses us. He looks like a Dalmatian cross and if he or his fellow residents get wind of the fact that we're passing on the lane, they'll soon get into an eager fit of barking to attract our attention. All of them will be wagging their tails, but this one in particular will immediately grab his aluminium feed dish, which is probably larger than a dinner plate, and leap atop his kennel. He'll then try and make as much noise as he can, but without dropping the dish from his jaw.

Agapitos has an old pickup, it's a white Ford and must be twenty years old if it's a day. Most old Greeks around here (and probably nationwide) allow their pickups to degenerate into a worse and worse state until they are seriously unroadworthy, or at least look as if they are. Not so with Agapitos. His pickup is always clean and the tyres always have plenty of tread on them. His rear number plate sports the sticker that proves that the KTEO roadworthiness test which must be done every two years after a vehicle reaches four years of age is up to date. He's an exception to the general rule and no mistake.

He's an affable guy who always has time to stroll over to the fence when we walk past. It's a dust lane quite some distance from anywhere, but it happens to be the route we take when walking from home down to the beach for a swim, a habit that we acquired shortly after coming out here to live. He'll usually be bent double over his vegetables, or perhaps sitting on his diesel rotavator, the kind that's like a mini-tractor with a seat for the driver, as he turns over the soil around his olive trees once the rains have begun.

When he has produce, he'll invariably want to be sure that we don't pass by without being presented with some of it. We don't mind at all. He's a white-haired wiry guy who's probably well into his seventies, but he's no push-over. A couple of years ago a local businessman who owns several large nearby hotels came up the hill, well, sent someone else up the hill, with a clutch of rebars and a tape measure and began driving the rebars into the ground in a pattern that clearly said:

"I'm going to enclose this area".

The only trouble was, the bars were driven into the ground in such a manner as to threaten the boundary of Agapitos' allotment, and also to re-route the lane for several hundred metres, thus depriving him of any access to his ktima. When we ambled past one day and asked if he knew what it was all about, having seen these rebars suddenly springing up all across the landscape, he replied that the businessman, who's well known in the area, wanted to construct either another hotel to add to his ever-expanding portfolio, or perhaps a string of villas to let to tourists during the summer season. Either way, the plan was to deprive old Agapitos of his nice little allotment, re-route a public access lane that had been in situ for centuries and plough up and concrete over a fairly extensive stretch of virgin land in the name of tourism.

Agapitos was having none of it. He quickly alerted a fellow landowner who owned a *ktima* through which the villain of the piece wanted to send the re-routed lane and the two of them got a couple of lawyers to spring into action. Within a week Agapitos had strapped a series of signs to the fence around his allotment [ktima]. These consisted of the plastic tops of those big round tubs with wire handles that emulsion comes in, each with what looked like a target painted on it in red and blue. There was also an arrow in black and a number. We asked him what these meant and he told us that they spelt out in clear terms exactly where his land ended, and it was further out than merely the fence around his allotment. The lane too was his for about a hundred metres, the exact section of the lane that the enemy wanted to re-route elsewhere. If he'd had his way the hotelier would have brought the wall of one of his proposed new buildings right up to within inches of Agapitos' fence and in the same instance deprived the old farmer of access to his property.

Unfortunately, it's still the case here that someone with enough clout, ie. cash, can virtually do whatever he wants. Forget restrictions about where one can and can't build, forget ancient rights of way, if the right wad of cash is slipped into the right hands, things happen. Legal obstacles mysteriously disappear. As it happened in this case, the aggressive businessman was from the same village as the two guys whose noses he was putting out of joint. In the end the potential family problems and his risk of losing respect in the village came to the rescue of the two probable victims. Before long the ominous rebars either got bent or mysteriously disappeared. We still have our lane to walk along and old Agapitos still greets us at the fence and passes the time of day with us.

Crucially, we still arrive home with courgettes, tomatoes and eggs now and again too.

There are so many other people we now consider friends who just over a decade ago we never knew. For example there's Athanasia, who's permanently behind the kitchen counter at taverna Agapitos (her husband's name, not the same chap as just discussed above, although of course they are related). She not only spends probably 90% of her time fixing *Ellinikos* for the domino and backgammon playing men of the village, but also sorts and stores the mail for a fairly large number of folk who live in the surrounding area.

Athanasia is quite short, built for comfort rather than speed and is always dressed in dark brown. She permanently has an apron adorning her body and never ceases to greet me with kindness and civility. She must now be in her mid-fifties, since she looked as if she was when we first arrived in 2005. As is often the case with Greek marriages, hubby Agapitos is probably at least ten years her senior and he busies himself about the place tending the plants in the steeply sloping garden below their taverna's terrace and generally keeping the outdoor areas in good repair. From their terrace you can enjoy a spectacular view down the long valley to the sea about five kilometres below. When we first came the taverna, which serves as a kafeneion in the morning hours, used to be an official sub-post office. There was a modest

ELTA [Greek Post Office] sign at the bottom of the steps leading up to the terrace and a desk provided by ELTA in the rear corner of the room, separated from the kitchen by the back door, outside of which there is always a stack of crates containing perhaps beer bottles or cans of soft drinks. Maybe empties too.

 On top of, behind and in front of the desk was a seemingly permanent pile of packages, usually brown cardboard, many with all kinds of logos printed in black on their sides, logos like Amazon, DSL etc. Stacked in piles on the desk were wads of letters wrapped in thick brown elastic bands and a jumble of jiffy bags of various shapes and sizes. Doubtless the packages would be collected, but to me each time I went the four kilometres up the valley to see Athanasia and collect our mail, the piles looked the same. All of the population of the village of Asklipio collects its mail from here. So, in addition to running the kafeneion/taverna all day every day, Athanasia was a sub-postmistress too. Apart from those living in the village, which has a population of around 700, many people from the area of Kiotari also go there to collect their mail. The nearest real full-time post office is located in the village of Gennadi, but unless you have about three weeks to spare and take along a Thermos and a sleeping bag, maybe a tent too, you wouldn't want your mail ending up there awaiting collection. OK, maybe I'm using hyperbole here, but last time I went to the Gennadi post office I came home needing another shave.

 A few years ago the sub-post office was terminated due to cuts being made by ELTA. At first everyone who collected their mail from Athanasia was depressed at the prospect of having to place even more strain on the shoulders of the poor girl who sits behind the counter at the Gennadi office. Not to mention the delightful prospect of having to lose the best part of a day just to post a letter or collect one's mail. Pretty soon though it was business as usual. One by one we began asking Athanasia if she'd carry on holding our mail for us because, under the new arrangement, Mr. Kyriakos from the Gennadi office would be coming up to the Agapitos three times one week and twice the next, to sit at a table and serve as a mobile post office for an hour or so. Of course, he'd be served the regulation Elliniko while he worked, on the house.

I've been up there when he comes. He's a big, burly man with a ready smile and is good natured enough. He waltzes into the Agapitos at around 1.30pm, well, more like any time between then and 3.00pm, depending on what distractions may have affected his schedule on that particular day. He carries a heavy, well-worn thick leather satchel over his shoulder which he swings around to rest on his knees when he first sits down. Out of the satchel he draws one of those little metal sprung coin-holders (they hold several denominations) and a rubber stamp and ink pad. Various official ELTA forms are also produced, some of them in book form, some loose. After three or four minutes he's ready to do business with the clutch of local folk (mainly men) that's gathered around him. The last thing he draws out from his satchel (it's a big satchel) will be a wad of mail, bundles of letters held by elastic bands and stacks of current bills, usually for electricity and telephone accounts. Satellite TV and water bills also figure now and then.

If there are any packets to deliver he'll either drop his satchel and return down the steep steps to his car below to retrieve them, or he'll get one of the more spritely of his eager customers to do it, which can be quite a difficult choice, owing to the physical condition of the majority of them, many of whom took probably a quarter of an hour to get up the steps in the first place.

People can pay their bills with him, just as they would at the actual Post Office, plus send all kinds of mail. He even carries a portable set of electronic scales so that he can calculate what to charge if you want to send a package from there. Mr. Kyriakos knows by heart all the names of folk who either live in Asklipio or of others in the surrounding area who, like us, prefer to have our mail sent to Asklipio. Thus we hatched the idea of asking him if he'd continue to leave our mail with Athanasia even if we weren't present when he came for one of his visits. He was only too pleased to oblige.

"As long as *Kyria* Athanasia agrees," he told me, which she did. So, after a couple of weeks of anxiety, everything soon returned to exactly as it was before she was deprived of her privilege of being a sub-postmistress. On some occasions, I even leave a letter with her to send when he comes and she's fine about that, often telling me not to pay her for the stamps until the next time I go up there.

In the more than ten years that we've lived here I only recall seeing Athanasia out and about in the area once. You know how it is when you always see someone in the same environment, in the same location and situation? You wouldn't fail to know them when you went there. After all, you'd expect that person to be a part of the scene when you arrive. Lift that person out of that familiar environment though, see them driving past in a car, bump into them in a store some distance away from where you normally see them and then you look at them, smile embarrassingly and attempt to acknowledge them, even hold a brief conversation, without having the faintest idea where you know them from.

Go on, admit it, you've been there.

When we saw Athanasia that one time, she was getting out of a car with her husband Agapitos, outside the Gré Café in Kiotari, which is run by the two Georges. Of course, there is a family relationship since they all come from the same village. Goes without saying, but if it hadn't been for the few words she spoke to us first I'd have embarrassed myself big-time.

A couple more people we've come to know really well are the two Georges, who are related to each other through marriage. "Little" (well, he's not so little and perhaps would best be described as 'shorter') George is married to Panagiota, whose mum is Stella and whose brother is the other "taller" George. Stella's hubby also helps out around the place. This lovely family has transformed a part of Kiotari that once had no heart.

The main road through Kiotari is, as my Dad used to say "nothing to write home about." There are a few quite large, but mercifully low-rise hotels, some tourist shops and little else. There is a kind of shopping precinct of very modest proportions almost opposite the Rodos Princess Hotel. It's built around a rectangular courtyard and houses Dimitri's Bar, which we've never patronised even once because, although it has nice comfy chairs, the only outlook from them is a few faceless shops in a courtyard about the size of a tennis court.

The premises now occupied by the Gré Café when we first came here were three walls of dirty glass panes, inside of which sat a selection of forlorn and deserted terracotta plant pots that no one seemed worried about leaving there forever. We'd go for our regular walks and every time we passed that empty building we'd bemoan the fact that there was no café/bar in the area and how great it would be if someone took it on and turned it into one.

After we'd been here five or six years work began and we would go past with our curiosity piqued and peer into the place at the work as it progressed, ever hoping that it would become a café. The rest is history. Development has gone on at quite a pace since then and now there is another bar right next door, a completely new build and slightly bigger and flashier than the two Georges' Gré Café, and called "Ipanema". Of course the Georges (and us) know the owner well as he's also an Asklipian. At first they were worried that the newer, dare I say "flashier" Ipanema would be the death of them, but it hasn't worked out that way. The Ipanema is much more tourist-friendly in that it looks every inch the cocktail bar, whereas the Georges' place is a down-home coffee/snack bar. What's actually happened is the other shops (including a couple of new ones) plus the Ipanema have increased the "footfall" (oh yeah, I know all the phrases they use in the trade) and the Gré Café has thrived and increased its business.*

Further down the road lives Akis the druggy plumber. He's a nice bloke but can't seem to get himself clean of drugs. He used to be an excellent plumber and was very much in demand, but in the past few years his work has dried up as he acquired a reputation for starting jobs, cadging cash from his customers, disappearing somewhere to buy his next fix and never going back to finish the work.

It came as a shock to us when we found out about the drug problems here. Not just in Rhodes town is there a problem, but in villages such as Gennadi, butter-wouldn't-melt traditional villages that tourists stop off at while doing their island tours in their little hire cars. They'll turn into the village, park up in the square, walk around for a while and drink a beer or a coffee in the traditional kafeneion, take a few photos and set off again, entirely ignorant of the fact that down on certain patches of the nearby beach one can turn up at the crack of dawn very often and see the evidence of the previous nights' druggy gathering. There are syringes, the remains of fires that were lit from driftwood, empty beer bottles and other stuff I wouldn't want to describe here. Seems some aspects of the modern world have fingers that reach very far into the otherwise idyllic places that we all love to visit for our dream holiday.

I suppose that last point well illustrates what I said at the top of this chapter. People are basically the same the world over, right?

* *Since completing this chapter the Gré Café has bought out the Ipanema, so that the two businesses now operate under the name Gré Café*

11. A Bunch of Stuff

I locked us out once. Something we had to get used to quickly was the way the Greeks fit the locks to the doors on the majority of properties these days. Our place has a set of French Windows, which don't have a handle on the outside at all, so you can only open them from indoors. Apart from these we have only one front door, which is a nice modern white aluminium affair with a fixed handle on the outside for pulling it shut, plus a keyhole for the… well, for the front door key. The fixed handle doesn't move. It doesn't operate the bolts built into the door and frame. Its sole purpose is to facilitate the pulling of the door to close it when desired.

On the inside of the front door there's a proper lever handle, so no problems there then. When we lived in the UK the last couple of properties we lived in had new uPVC doors and windows (which we ourselves had ordered and had fitted) and when you get your nice new front door it usually has a lever handle on the outside as well as on the inside. You can pull the door to, turn the handle upwards to engage the bolts and leave it like that without actually locking it with the key. This means you can potter about in the garden and just pop back inside with a simple grab of the handle, turning it downward. Hey presto, the door opens.

Out here they still use aluminium in preference to uPVC. I've never actually asked anyone but I theorise that the uPVC system wouldn't work over here due to the intense heat during the summer months. No doubt it would suffer from all kinds of problems from warping, maybe even melting. So they stick with the aluminium type, usually finished in white which means that they look very much like the British uPVC ones before you make a closer inspection.

The front doors can so very often only be opened if you have the key on you. Pull the door to without the key and you're locked out. If you've another way of entering the building then you'll probably have little need to begin tearing your hair out, but if the only other set of doors you have are French doors without a handle on the outside, and they happen to be closed and locked, then you wouldn't want to be pulling your front door closed behind you if you didn't have the key sticking out of the keyhole to facilitate re-entry, or perhaps a key about your person.

Plus, if you've been daft enough to insert the key into the keyhole on the interior side of the door, then this prevents a key from being inserted on the outside. So say, for example, you have a spare key hidden somewhere outdoors for just such an eventuality: that is, you've pulled the front door closed and you haven't got the key inserted into the outside lock on the door or have a key about your person, that spare key won't be any good to you because, if there's already a key on the inside then the one on the outside will not, it will simply refuse to, go into that lock. Thus, you're locked out. You have no way of getting back into the house.

Of course, sensible people don't insert a key into the lock on the interior side of the door unless possibly they're already indoors and planning on retiring for the night. Sensible people, when they're hanging about the house during the daytime, will always have a key protruding from the exterior lock on their front door so that they can let themselves back in when they want a cuppa. Maybe something stronger. Sensible people over here never simply leave the door wide open, because the huge variety of "livestock" that lives out here and gets very active during the warm summer months will soon colonise your lounge and start giving you serious grief later on when it's dark and you're hoping for a peaceful night's sleep. Such livestock may include a few benevolent creatures like geckos, but invariably it will also include the dreaded mosquito, plus all kinds of other things that are next to invisible but always get active late in the evening and begin feasting on your exposed flesh.

Thus you get into the habit of keeping your doors closed and the mozzy nets in place across those of your windows that you leave open to air the place.

It's during the evening, especially during the evening in winter time when it gets dark much earlier, not to mention quite chilly too, that you close and lock all your windows, light the log-burner and, when it gets near to bed time, we have the habit of taking the front door key out from the exterior keyhole and placing it in the interior one, where we'll also turn the key to operate the deadbolt, thus preventing anyone getting in overnight. I'm not saying that security and crime are huge issues here, but there's no harm in being careful anyway.

The night we got locked out was during the winter. We'd been entertaining Petros and Lena, who got a mention in chapter 10 of volume three in the Ramblings From Rhodes series, *"Tzatziki For You To Say"*. Petros it was who was very proud of himself for shipping their washing machine and cooker over here from Canada when they moved back to Rhodes a couple of decades ago. Both appliances are huge (they still have them, now, about seventeen years on) when you reflect on the amount of space that your average housewife has to play with in a Canadian suburban home. Their utility room alone back in Canada was probably half the size of our entire living area here in Rhodes. The average washing machine over there is a huge great top-loading tub, very different from the front-loading compact 500mm wide appliances favoured by Europeans. In my previous account I mentioned the fact that they'd had a mechanical problem with the washing machine, which was probably manufactured by General Electric or something like that, so Petros had stripped it down and discovered what the problem was.

He'd then ordered the replacement parts through his brother back in Toronto and paid a small fortune both for the parts and for shipping them from Canada to Rhodes. Petros evidently couldn't work out the fact that he could have bought a much more modern machine up the road here in Rhodes, got a three year warranty with it too, and all for less that he'd paid to repair the huge beast that he'd brought all the way from Canada and which belonged even then (seven years ago) on a rubbish tip.

The victory in his mind was the fact that he'd beaten the villains who manufacture appliances with built-in 'planned obsolescence' by fixing a washing machine that was a couple of decades old. Hah! That showed 'em.

Anyway, they'd been over for an evening's *"parea"* (socialising) and very nice it had been too. For some odd reason either my wife or I had stuck the front door key on the inside of the door, as if we'd not be opening it again before the next morning. As if we'd planned to go to bed in fact. It was probably done unconsciously by either my better half or I, although in the interests of point-scoring I took the blame for what happened later.

Point-scoring? Come on chaps, you know what I mean. By taking this on the chin and accepting liability I could use it to my advantage on another occasion. Perhaps another day we'd be planning to go out, maybe with an arrangement to be somewhere at, say 8.00pm. At 7.55pm, when the good woman is still titivating her face in front of the dressing table mirror and we've still got a twenty minute drive in front of us to reach our destination for the evening, it's at such a moment when I can use my points, see?

"You're never ready on time. You never allow yourself enough time to get ready." I could say, for example. She'd doubtless counter with,

"It's not my fault. You distracted me, asking me to do thus and so," or perhaps, "if you hadn't used all the hot water in the shower…" That kind of thing. Then, fellas, you can use your ace in the hole.

"Didn't I admit it when I got us locked out that time? See, I can admit it when I'm in the wrong."

And so on and so forth.

Anyway, we'd had a great evening's anecdote-telling and having a good laugh over a beautiful meal and a glass of Metaxa afterwards. Time came for our guests to leave and I arose to see them out. My wife fetched their coats and we began the usual round of double cheek-kissing and hugs before seeing them out of the front door.

I could have sworn in a court of law that I'd suggested to my wife that she stay in the warm while I opened the garden gate for our guests to drive out. She doesn't remember that bit. So, as I drew the gate to a close as they peeped their horn and drove carefully off down the lane, I didn't think anything of it when, as I closed the gate my wife was standing beside me, also waving into the darkness through which it was extremely doubtful our friends could see the gesture.

We turned and walked the twenty metres or so back on to our terrace and toward the front door. On reaching the front door and finding it closed, with no key in the exterior lock, I said,

"You did bring the key out with you, didn't you?"

"I thought you had it." She replied.

"No, I told you to stay inside while I saw them off. So if you've come out I assume that you'd have taken the key out from the inside and brought it out with you. Don't tell me…"

Her face replied. She'd not looked at the key in the inside lock, she'd decided that since I was outside then I must have brought the key out with me. I, on the other hand, had thought I was safe in the knowledge that I could leave the key where it was because my wife would still be inside the house after I'd seen off our guests. Quite often we pull the door to as it were, bringing it to an almost closed position without actually engaging the latch. In such circumstances it looks closed at first glance, but can still be pushed open without a problem. My first thought was that this would be what she'd done.

I was wrong. She'd pulled the door completely closed in order to, according to her explanation, keep the heat in, while we saw Petros and Lena off. Whatever, when we reached the front door it was firmly closed and the key was in the lock on the inside of the door. It was very late in the evening and very dark outside. At least we had left a couple of exterior lights on.

After we'd blamed each other for the problem, I decided to go and find our spare key, secreted somewhere in the garden, and give it a try. You know how sometimes you're sure about something, but because you're in a fix you still decide that the something you're usually sure about may just, in this instance, be perhaps something that you ought to doubt? What I'm trying to say is, I of course already knew that if the key was in the inside lock, then the spare key wouldn't be able to go into the exterior one. In circumstances such as this, however, you allow your earnest wish to take over from logic, from what you know is going to be the case, and clutching at straws you go and try something that you know will never work. At that point in time, however, you just entertain that vain hope that for just this once the laws of nature will be slightly more flexible than normal.

All this flashing through my mind, I dashed into the garden, retrieved the spare front door key and marched over to the offending, firmly closed door and tried to shove the key into the lock. I knew that with the key on the inside it wouldn't work, but short of any other alternatives I did it in the vain hope that a shift in the space-time continuum would allow me just this once to get away with it and the key would slide gracefully all the way in and I'd be able to open the door. Crisis over.

Right first time. The key went part-way in and then reality hit me with both barrels. No way would there be an exception to the rule. Key on the inside means no key goes in on the outside. The law of inevitability. Of course, despite knowing it was futile, I withdrew the key and tried again…and again…and again. Each time the same result. The key would not go all the way in and the lock resolutely refused to turn.

We were locked out.

"Why not call Petros on his mobile? They won't be too far away yet." The beloved said.

"Great idea. Maybe he'll have some suggestions, at least some ideas about how we can get back in." I replied, "Give us your mobile phone then."

"Haven't you got yours on you?" She asked. We both already knew the answer to that one. Both of our mobile phones were inside the house, on the telephone shelf a few inches from the front door.

"We must have left at least one window unlocked, surely." I said and set off for a tour of the exterior of the house to see what I could find. Without exception all the windows were locked and their blinds pulled almost to a close. After we'd just begun to experience that feeling of panic that yelled "this is going to cost us!" I remembered that I hadn't checked the bathroom window. All the windows in our bedroom, kitchen area and lounge/dining room are virtually flush with the exterior walls and their lower sills no higher than my waist. The bathroom window, however, is at least my eye-height from the ground and much smaller than all the others. It's only about two feet wide by about eighteen inches deep and its mosquito screen is the only one in the house that's fixed to the frame and doesn't slide along. All the others cover 50% of the window area because the windows are dual sliding sashes, thus only one of them can be open at any one time. You just slide the mozzie screen to the left or right, depending on which side you've opened. The bathroom window is a single pane that opens with an interior handle and swings inwards on hinges. Its mozzie net is set in a white aluminium frame that's screwed to the exterior window frame with screws that have a special head, designed to prevent an intruder from having an easy time of unscrewing them in order to break in.

Add to all this the fact that the window is set deeply back with a 'reveal' of about fifteen inches and you begin to see our dilemma. The idea of us sleeping in the car for the night was beginning to sound realistic. Except this was winter, the temperature was dropping and we weren't dressed for the outdoors.

Sometimes things turn out better than you could have dreamed they would. After we'd got over our initial irritation at each other, both having decided that the other was to blame for our dilemma, and of course I'd then accepted the blame for not having put the key in the outside of the door when I went outside with our guests to see them off (even though I was sure I'd told the beloved to stay indoors in the warm and thus felt that there was no need to worry about the key), there was the welcome sight of a pair of car headlamps coming up the lane. Could it be Petros and Lena coming back for some odd reason? We hadn't been able to call them so they couldn't have had any idea that us two chumps were sitting at the patio table entering the first stages of hypothermia.

Yes, they'd come back because Lena had only gone and left her handbag on our sofa. How handy was that? Petros also had a few tools in the back of his car and was soon able to give me a leg-up so that I could reach the screws holding the mozzie net in place over the bathroom window, which, joy of joys, we'd indeed left ajar, phew. The screwdriver he proffered wasn't the right one for the strangely shaped heads on the screws holding the screen in place. But it was good enough to loosen them and I was then able to unscrew them the rest of the way by hand. I felt distinctly like an intruder breaking into the window of my own home, but the sense of relief I felt when I eventually tumbled to the floor in the bathroom was something else. Once inside and only slightly bruised by my window-wriggle-through and my five-foot fall to the tiled bathroom floor, I was at the front door in thirty seconds and threw it open with a feeling of relief the like of which I haven't experience often in my life. Maybe once or twice when we've stopped the car up in the mountains so that I could leap out and run behind a bush would also qualify.

Needless to say, ever since that night we've been doubly careful about where we put the key and never go outside without being sure to insert it into the exterior lock before closing the door.

The mention of the reasons for not leaving one's front door open brings to mind the adjustments one has to make when it comes to understanding the wildlife and vegetation of this country. The flora and fauna if you like. The worst you can expect in the UK if you leave your windows open is maybe a bee, a wasp, perhaps a few bluebottles. In our last home before we left the UK, down in deepest South Wales in the village of St. Athan, we'd had a loft conversion bedroom installed in our bungalow which meant that we would sleep with our bed right beneath a Velux window. You could tilt open the Velux about six inches along the bottom edge, which we'd frequently do during the summer months when the nights were termed 'mild' by the TV weather forecasters, with temperatures holding up at something into the teens Celsius. There were no such things as mosquito nets, and no fear of nasty flying things that may wish to dine on your exposed flesh coming in during the night.

Here it's a different story. You sleep with windows open only if you have them screened with a mosquito net. Something we soon began to discover here though was that these nets aren't much good at preventing the "flying full-stops" from coming in (Americans call them 'No-see-ums'). The insect life here, especially the flying versions, seem designed to cause you maximum distress. Mozzies themselves are hideous things. I'm sure they have a very important role to play in keeping the environment in balance, but they damn well sure are keen to go above and beyond the call of duty. Get just one, yes just one of these abominations inside your room at night and you'll either wake up next morning with red welts all over the place, or you'll be up half the night trying to kill the thing.

But Mozzies are pussycats compared to the "flying full-stops". I call them that because I have no other word for them. I have no idea what they're called by people who study such things, but they're so small that they can simply cruise through the mesh of your mozzie net and, unless one flits across your line of sight while you're lounging about late at night, you won't be aware of their presence until they set about their work of nipping any exposed area of flesh that you may be unfortunate enough to have left exposed from under the sheet on your bed. You may be enjoying the late evening warmth either outside or in during the summer months, but these little sadists come out after sundown intent solely on making you itch. Because they're so small you only notice that they've got you when you start unconsciously scratching your arm, or perhaps your leg, maybe your neck even – in several places. We hadn't been here long when I began to wonder what was wrong. What was going on? How come I was finding these little 'Ayers Rocks' coming up on my legs, my arms, elsewhere too? Their presence is alarming enough, but when you add to that the fact that they itch with an intensity that makes you want to scratch it raw, you can very soon wonder if you've caught the plague or something.

It took me a long time to eventually conclude that it was these tiny 'flying full-stops' that were the cause of my misery. At first I simply thought it was mosquitos. It was only after weeks of night time misery, when we'd become quite sure that there were no mozzies penetrating our defences, that we realised that it had to be something else. Gradually we 'got our eye in' as it were and began to notice these miniscule villains. It was then that I resolved to do two things, **one:** to use insect repellent and **two:** to always keep a supply of Lanes Tea Tree and Witch Hazel Cream in our first aid drawer. That cream is simply amazing. It's recently been marketed under a different name, it seems that the manufacturers Lanes now (in their infinite wisdom) call it *"Teangi"* - don't ask me why. Seems a pointless exercise to me. One thing I do know, rub it in where you've got an itchy bite and within minutes the itching disappears. That's all I need to know.

By and large me and the beloved are very environmentally conscious, we don't like using chemicals. For this reason my wife never uses sprays around the house, no aerosol furniture polish, air fresheners, none of that kind of stuff. If we can use something natural, then we will. When it comes to keeping the dreaded biting insects at bay though, I give up. I surrender. Give me the chemicals. Spray me all over, anything to stop that damned itching. OK, to temper that a little, we do try and use citronella where possible. In fact, in the garden we have some lemon geraniums and they're pretty good at doing the job too. Seems after Googling it that ours are the Mabel Grey Sherbert Lemon variety (all you need now is a stick of liquorice, eh?). Their leaves smell very strongly of lemon. In fact, when I'm gardening now I pluck a few leaves, bruise them and then rub them on my arms and face, legs too if I'm in my shorts (sorry about that mental picture you've just conjured up) and within minutes the flying terrors start giving me a wide berth. Good tip there folks. Trust me, it works.

Other creatures that may tend to wander into your front room if you leave a door or window open without a net over here may include some pretty impressive spiders, scorpions, tree frogs and a variety of lizards. If they're geckos, we're fine with that. In fact, for the last couple of summers we've had a gecko or two living under the sofa and that's cool. They're like nature's vacuum cleaners. They'll come out when you've tootled off to bed and they'll roam the floors and walls in search of spiders and anything that may have six legs which may be taking a little time out on the surface. The only slight drawback can be if you get up to go to the loo in the dark. I'd suggest you don't do it without some level of lighting being employed. I've come that close to treading on a gecko on more than one occasions that it worries me. They're such cute little bods, they really are. Most of them are almost translucent like a little piece of orangy-brown Play-Doh and can easily blend in to the markings on your floor tiles, especially if they're brown, orange or grey. The tiles that is, not the… oh, you understand.

Scorpions are generally to be avoided. The type we get over here aren't particularly large, measuring usually only about two inches, but they can certainly put you in hospital if they sting you. They have the habit of lurking under things in dark crevices. If you're shifting stones in the garden, for example, don't ever just shove your fingers underneath one to lever it away from the soil. That's the ideal lurking place for scorpions. If you're clearing leaf litter it's also not a good idea to use your bare hands. Me and the better half have never yet been stung, but we know several people who have and it's extremely painful and at the very least they ended up in the local medical centre for treatment. If, however, you employ the basic safety methods, like using a trowel to flick a stone over before attempting to pick it up, not shoving your bare hands into organic litter in small corners, not even lifting a sunbed from the place where perhaps it's lain in storage for a few weeks, you'll probably be just fine.

The other peril when it comes to picking up stones is that they often have a spider's web on the underside. Not a web like you'd normally imagine, but rather a 'pod' of white silk that's almost impossible to see through. It'll be an inch or so across, sometimes more, but can all too often still be inhabited by an eight-legged fiend that, once disturbed, can end up running up your arm, looking far too big to have been concealed in that silky purse.

Of course, we have a few native species of snake here as well. We haven't yet had one in the house, but we know people who have. It's quite common to walk the gravel paths in the garden or the dusty dirt lanes that criss-cross the hillsides here and see the familiar pattern that shows that a snake has slithered across the way some time before you got there. The beloved is terrified of confronting one, but to be honest, they hear human footfall a long time before we get close enough to see one most of the time and they'll slither away into the undergrowth, reluctant to encounter a human from close quarters. There is one fairly impressive species though. I don't know what they call it, but it's predominantly black, can be an inch or two thick and up to four feet long. We have been driving up or down our kilometre of lane on several occasions and come across one of these basking on the dust in the sunshine. As we've approached in the car the snake has casually woken up, taken a disdainful glance toward the car and then proceeded to casually slither off into the vegetation to the side of the lane, doing its utmost to look miffed at having its sunbathing session curtailed while we've waited with the car in neutral before proceeding on our way. I've been told that the black ones are harmless. I've no idea if that's right, but I hope so, because on a few occasions it's looked very much like a couple are living in our garden, not all that far from the house.

I installed an irrigation system as we developed the garden. If you're a regular visitor to Greece you'll doubtless have seen that nearly every garden has such a system. They're a virtual necessity during the long dry summer months. You'll see black pipes snaking (good pun, eh? I may not be Tim Vine, but now and again I come close) across the beds, punctuated by either red or black nozzles which dispense the water to the base of each plant. It's a very good idea and much more 'green' than simply watering with a hose or can, since no water is wasted, it all goes to the spot where it's needed. Plus it means that the number of weeds that grow elsewhere during the dry months is greatly reduced because there's no moisture for them to grow in.

As a result of having installed our system, I often make adjustments as we move plants around, put new ones in, or take dying ones out. The upshot of this is that I often leave lengths of the black piping laying around while I make the adjustments to the system. A few years back I was standing at the back of the car port, where we'd left a couple of white PVC sun loungers stacked up beside the car. I was probably spraying one of our hibiscus bushes with a solution of soapy water, since it's apparently a green way of getting rid of aphids. We get the occasional infestation of blackfly on the hibiscus. As I stood there I remember seeing a length of what I thought was black irrigation pipe out of the corner of my eye, on the floor beneath these two sun loungers, not three feet from where I was standing.

You can imagine how it fazed me when this length of pipe began to move of its own accord. At first it was disbelief that kept me standing there, but after a millisecond or two it dawned on me that this piece of piping was not in fact a piece of piping at all, but a four-foot long black snake that had been basking on the hot paviours. It was in one way a good experience for me, because the snake slithered off away from me, side-wound across the car port right under the car (leaving me at first in a near-panic over what I'd have done if it had decided to take up residence in the engine bay) and set off up the steep bank at the back of the patio behind the car port. Once you get about four or five feet up the bank there is thick undergrowth into which the snake disappeared, gradually. It was that long that it seemed to me to take half an hour for all of it to become concealed. I've since seen it in the vicinity several times, thus leading me to conclude that it's living up there somewhere. The fact was though, that it fled from me. My wife thinks they're all lurking around waiting for their opportunity to wind themselves around her and crush the life out of her. Either that or they're just dying to lunge at her foot and plunge their fangs into her shins. The fact is though, they just want to keep out of our way.

That's just as well, because on another occasion while we were eating lunch on the terrace, a brown one slithered across the path between the two flower beds at the front of the house, probably eight feet from our toes. The brown ones, plus some grey ones so I've been told, are altogether much more dangerous than the larger but more innocuous black ones. If one of those bites you, be sure your last will and testament are current. Well, I may be overdoing it a tad, but that would certainly be true if you already had some ongoing health issue. If, though, you're in strapping health, then a short stay in hospital should sort you out.

Tree frogs are here in abundance. Now these are a different kettle of fish. I suppose it's a bit awful to contemplate the thought that they serve as elevenses for a lot of the snakes, but on the other hand they keep the insect and spider population in check too. They're really cute, quite beautiful to look at and have the habit of coming on to peoples' terraces and scaling their walls overnight. We know of one couple whom we visit now and again, whose canopy-covered terrace is a real haven for the tree frogs. You can sit there sipping your drink of a morning and see a couple of them sitting eight feet up on the top of the light fitting that is fixed to the wall above the patio doors. There are a couple of glazed ceramic jardinières on the terrace too and very often there will be a tree frog or two sitting on top of the stand section, just around the edge of the pot. How on earth they get there I can't imagine.

I could go on and on listing the wildlife that one gets used to here, much of which is quite harmless I'm sure, like the tree frogs. It still can give you a bit of a shock though. Lots of folk have the habit of leaving shoes outside their front doors overnight. We do it often. I mean, think about it. If you've spent a few hours with your feet in a pair of trainers in temperatures hovering around the forty Celsius mark, you're not going to want to put those shoes in your cupboard right away without giving them an airing, now are you?

Anyone who's lived here a while will be in the habit of giving their shoes a bash before putting them on in the morning. I can't be the only person who's discovered the hard way that a three inch locust might be having an overnight kip in the toe-end of one of my trainers. At least not wearing socks does away with the possibility of a gooey mess ending up all over one of them.

Something that delights us absolutely is the fact that there are not only deer on the island, but there are lots of them living in our valley. Back in 2008, when the huge fires raged here, the deer population was devastated. Hunting in all its forms was banned in this area for a period of three years. Not that the hunters are supposed to hunt deer anyway, but I've seen evidence of that particular regulation not being adhered to. No, hunters, who aren't all that clever at keeping to the legal hunting season either, are supposed to be after quail, rabbits, hares maybe. As the years have passed since the fires, the deer population has recovered to the extent that now, during the winter months, we see them on almost a daily basis. Sometimes, when we go foraging in the hills with the chainsaw for some wood for the log-burner, we'll come face to face with a few stags and does, who'll stand there and watch us with curious eyes before they decide to either trot off and leave us alone, or continue grazing.

I asked a Greek friend how come there are deer on the island anyway. I don't know why but we hadn't expected them here. If you've been to Rhodes then you can't have failed to notice the two stone columns standing either side of the entrance to Mandraki Harbour in Rhodes Town. Atop one is a magnificent antlered stag and atop the other is a doe. The species here is a modestly sized type of fallow deer and the story goes that they were introduced to the island, probably in the middle ages, to reduce the snake population, which was quite bothersome to humans at the time. How were deer meant to combat snakes though? Must confess, it didn't make much sense to me. But then, what do I know?

Theories include the idea that the deer would impale snakes on their antlers, maybe trample them to death with their hooves, eat them perhaps, or repel them with the odour of their urine. Some proffer the idea that deer droppings are poisonous to the snakes. Whatever is the case, apparently the strategy worked and the snake population was sufficiently reduced to the level at which they're no longer a major problem to humans living on the island.

I wonder if on reading this chapter you might just be thinking that it's a bit of a battle surviving here, what with all the 'livestock' that's intent on making life miserable, or even putting someone in hospital. I used to think about Australia in this light after I'd watched a TV documentary about the dreaded Red-back Spider, which apparently lurks on your car's sun-visor, ready to drop into your lap while you're driving and thus cause death either through having caused you to swerve off the road with shock and have a major accident or simply through the nasty little blighter biting you. Then I took a step back and thought, hold on, lots of people survive in Australia, even go on about how great it is to live there.

It's a bit like that with Rhodes. I often even now look at the locals while I'm nursing another nasty bite on my arm or leg and think, they seem to survive OK. You hardly even see a Greek bothering to swat away a fly or mosquito. Flies, now I haven't even been there in this chapter. In the UK, they're a nuisance. Here they're not just a nuisance, they damn well bite you. As I've mentioned elsewhere, lots of people here (well, just about all of the ex-pats) have cats and dogs all over the place. If I'm honest, which I always am of course, we don't have a lot of flies around our place. Go visit someone who has dishes of pet food dotted about the place though and you'll sit there sipping your drink, trying to have a nice, pleasant natter about something and you'll suddenly feel a pain exactly as if someone's jabbed a pin into your skin. It'll be a fly biting you. Exposed pet food equals more flies. One essential tool for any patio here is one of those plastic fly-swatters, which every supermarket in the country sells. Sometimes we sit with friends and probably get bitten at least half a dozen times by bloody flies.

Hand me that can. Now!

12. Mind Your Language

Learning Greek, easy? Well, maybe not so. Tell you what though, at the risk of hammering away my point far too heavily, I don't have a lot of sympathy for ex-pats, most of whom have lots of time on their hands, who don't at least have a go.

I'm the first to admit that coming here to live I had a bit of a head start on many. My mother-in-law was Greek and for thirty years or so before moving to Rhodes I'd had quite a lot of contact with my wife's Greek relatives and thus picked up what I used to call "taverna Greek". I knew just enough to get me into trouble. Now, in our twelfth year here, I know easily enough to do so.

First and foremost you need a healthy dose of humility. If you don't like being corrected then you won't get anywhere. If someone does correct you, and in my case it's more often than not my wife, you need to listen, thank them and try to apply what they tell you. Of course chaps, when it's your wife, the first reaction you feel welling up from within is self-justification. Resist that at all costs in this case. Most men reading this, though, will probably not have a Greek wife anyway and so the situation isn't likely to arise.

I suppose I should be grateful for my inherent nature. I'm a stubborn git and don't give up easily. I'm a very positive person and always tend to look forward, not back. For some people, sitting among Greek company for evening after evening would induce them to throw in the towel and go looking for some Brits with whom to sip their beer and talk about football. That's exactly how not to learn a new language. How did we learn our mother tongue? Let's be honest, most humans learn their own language while sitting on the floor as a toddler (OK, with all this health and safety mania these days, I should say 'in one's playpen'), playing with their bricks, doll (not in my case, all right? Despite what you may think) or perhaps on old egg-box, and hearing all the grown-ups talking around them. Soon we're taking our first tentative steps around the floor while saying "ma-ma ma-ma" to the ecstatic delight of our mother who then wants the rest of the world to hear their bairn's first attempts at communication. All of what's said around us goes into our ears and thus our brain and eventually it starts coming out through our mouths.

When we first came here my sister-in-law, who lived a couple of years in Athens when she was younger, told us, nay ordered us, to get a TV. She was, in fact, in Athens when I met my wife. Not when I met my wife as in, "I met her for lunch" or something. Rather, as in "when I met her for the first time", so she wouldn't then have actually been my wife just yet. That bit came later. You get the general idea.

Of course, I had no idea at the time, but when I met my wife Greece was under the rule of the Military Junta, which ran from 1967 until 1974. Things here were a bit edgy. Of course, I was a young impressionable hippie-in-the-making and had no idea about such things. All I knew was that there was this mysterious older sister whom I may one day meet, but when that day would come and what it might hold - I had no inkling. Apart, that is, from the dread that were the big sister to come home then my place in the life of my new girlfriend might face a serious threat, since the two girls, despite there being a five year age gap between them, had been quite the girls about town together before big sis had left for Greece.

Christine is my *Kounia'da*, meaning my wife's sister, as opposed to my brother's wife, who'd be my *ni'fi*. See now, you get the idea in cases like this just how tricky Greek can be. In English my wife's sister and my brother's wife are both my sisters-in-law. In Greek there's a distinction. It's further complicated by the fact that the word '*ni'fi*' also means 'bride'. But, ah ha, oh no, wait a minute, a man's daughter in law can also be his '*ni'fi*', which in English would make him sound like a bigamist. And by the way, while I'm on the subject, I don't have a brother.

Right. That all sorted? Good. So, I first met my wife in October 1971, when she was sweet sixteen and may have been kissed once or twice. I didn't want to ask. We'd been "going out" for a while before she told me that she had a sister. I'd met the two younger brothers, but it came as a bit of a shock when the news came out that there was this mysterious sister who lived in Athens and whom I had yet to meet. Since she was five years older than my new girlfriend, that made her also about four years older than me. Once she entered the scene I was soon appraised of the fact that, despite the relative youth of my significant other, she'd been on the nightclub scene with her sister for a while owing to the fact that she stood five eight, which meant she could get away with looking older. These days, of course, she gets away with looking a lot younger. In fact, it won't be long before people start thinking I'm out and about with my daughter, either that or I'm a cradle-snatcher.

We'd been an item for probably eighteen months when she broke the news to me that big sis was coming home. Her plans to stay in Greece had been shattered by the fact that the bloke she'd been engaged to marry, a certain Stefanos, had been two-timing her and it had broken her heart. Cheating bastard.

Anyway, when the time came for us to talk to her about our plans to move over here, she was a good person to ask about learning the language. We'd suggested that we wouldn't be wanting a TV over here. Christine, however, soon talked us out of that idea. We're glad she did because she was perfectly right about how it helps one learn the language, but also because all our dreamy ideas about evenings spent out of doors were wildly inaccurate when we found out during our first winter here that there are a couple of months during which it gets dark at 5.00pm-6.00pm and thus pretty cold outside too, so we'd be hard pressed to fill all those evenings without a TV to help us out.

Christine suggested that, even though we've never been the types to have the TV on in the background if we weren't actually watching it, as part of our efforts to learn Greek it might actually be a good idea. The theory is that the constant exposure to Greek being spoken would hasten our learning process, in exactly the same way as a toddler picks up its mother tongue through hearing it spoken around him/her all the time. Using radio would have a similar effect, except that when we first arrived out here our internet connection was relegated to dial up for a few years and back then there weren't any tablets (like iPads for example) around and even less apps like the ones you can get these days for listening to the radio on-line. The hi-fi only picked up one radio station here on the hillside where we live and it was a music station from Arhangelos. There were no talk stations to be had in deepest Kiotari.

The TV scores over radio too in that if you especially try and tune yourself in to the news programmes, you get all that scrolling text as well which you can practice reading while listening to the bulletin.

I'd made up my mind right from the off that I'd stick it out and spend as much time with Greek friends as I could, not resorting or reverting to English-speaking company any more than was required. I've never had a lesson in my life, but did use a couple of books in the beginning. One of these I'd still recommend to anyone. It was called "Learn Greek Without a

Teacher" and it's still available for order on line (*https://bibliagora.eu/learn-greek-without-a-teacher.html*).

Going back to the need for humility. If you're the kind of person who takes his or herself too seriously then you'll struggle. If you can laugh at yourself, you'll make progress. It's important to remember that in order to progress you have to speak, which means you'll make loads of mistakes along the way. When all those around you fall about it's also important to remember that they're not mocking you, they're simply reacting to something that's funny. OK, so it's something you said no doubt, but they'll usually be only too pleased to help you learn where you went wrong if you demonstrate your willingness to laugh along with them and then accept the correction.

So many times other ex-pats have said to me things like, "There's no point learning Greek, after all they all speak back to you in English." I mentioned in an earlier chapter about someone who believes that the Greeks don't even like you learning Greek. I strongly disagree. Come on folks, if you live in the UK or America, or wherever else in the world, you know that most people expect immigrants to learn the country's official language. Why should it be any different here in Greece, where frankly the island communities especially are worried about the influx of foreign nationals and the danger of this diluting the integrity of local communities?

Coming back to being humble. I'll illustrate now some of the pitfalls that it's all to easy to succumb to. See, the thing is, Greek is a very expressive language. It's far more expressive than English. There's no better way to illustrate this than with the word 'love'. Greek has four words for love. They are:

Storge – love between close relatives. *"Storgiko patera mou"* means my loving father.

Filia – love between friends, or those to whom you're not related. *'Philoxenia'* – love of strangers.

Erota, eros – Passionate love. *"Erotev'o"* fall in love.

Agapi – love based on principle.

In English, we have just the one word, love.

Then there are the 'cases'. These are perhaps the most thorny to grasp because they alter the spelling even of nouns and names depending on where in the sentence they occur. Modern Greek has four cases:

Nominative - for subjects of sentences.

Genitive - denoting possession.

Accusative - for objects (direct & indirect) of sentences.

Vocative - for calling (usually we call or talk to someone, but every object too has a vocative).

I'll just cite one example. The vocative is where you speak directly to someone. So, for example, Alex'andros, if I am addressing him directly, would be Alex'andre, that's the vocative. If I am talking about him, it will be Alex'andro, which would be the accusative. The nominative would be where he's the subject of the sentence, like, for example, Alex'andros is coming towards us. If I say Alex'andros' car in Greek, it would be the genitive, and should go like this: "*To autokinito tou Alexandrou.*" - the car of Alexandrou. Good eh?

What's also a potential minefield is the fact there is a pressing need to stress the correct syllable in Greek. Lots of words with the same spelling can be pronounced different ways with entirely different meanings. The easiest of these to use for illustrative purposes is the word *pote* [not ever pronounced poat (like as in boat) by the way]. This can be pronounced either *poh'-teh*, with the stress on the first syllable, meaning "when" in a question, or you can pronounce it *poh-teh'* stressing the second syllable and then it means "never". That's not even all there is to it either. For instance, if I want to ask a question about when Stavros is coming, I'll say "*poh'teh tha erthei o Stavros?*" - literally "when will come Stavros?, or as we'd say "when is Stavros coming?" But if I want to say "I'll be with you when I can", then the word for 'when' isn't *poh'teh* at all, it's *oh'tan*. Great, eh?

So, to the faut pas I've been guilty of over the years...

Only last week a knot of us were talking on a street corner and I told my wife and a friend to go and wait for me while I went and got the car. I suggested that they go "over there and wait for me on the parent." The Greek for 'corner' is '*gonyah*', while the Greek word for parent is '*goneyah*'. A simple mistake. Anyone can make it. Even my corners would have forgiven me for that one.

If you're in the bank and waiting in the queue, be careful not to do as I did and suggest to the bloke in the queue in front of me, when he began a friendly conversation to pass the time, that "it's a bit of a pain being in urine isn't it." The word for queue, or indeed tail (on an animal) is '*oorah*'' whereas the word for urine is '*oo'rah*'. Tricky.

When inviting someone for dinner it's far too easy to challenge them to come when you mean to invite them. I've also lost count of how many times I've suggested that I've arrived somewhere with my apron, when I actually mean that I've come on foot. If you're going out in the dark you may need to take a torch with you, not as I've so often suggested to Greek friends, take an envelope. I've been known to suggest that someone smells like another person when I actually meant to say that they resembled them. Something that could be extremely embarrassing – and I've fallen victim to it – is to suggest to some fella that he has a 'hard' when you mean he has a dog.

It's so easy to tell someone to pray when you actually want to suggest that they be careful. I've witnessed puzzled expressions on friends' faces when I've tried to say that I'd had a phone call when I'd actually said that I'd received a flight (as in a plane's flight). The word for meat is far too close to the word for debt. "What meat do I owe you?" one can very easily say after a favour when one wanted to say "how much" literally: "what debt…?"

A sure way to make people think you're obsessed with women's chestal regions is to suggest that you love athletics, when actually saying "Oh, I really enjoy breasts." It's not beyond the realms of possibility to go into a fabric store if you're thinking of making a pair of curtains and asking for some fertiliser. If someone's being obnoxious, be careful that you don't simply say "I don't like your conclusion" when you really wanted to say "I don't like your behaviour."

Three words that I perpetually have trouble remembering how to tell apart are the words for juice, anger and bulk (as in loose chippings from the builders' merchant). I've telephoned our local builders' yard, where fortunately they know me really well now, and asked for a ton of juice. When the bloke on the other end of the phone (after having shared the amusing moment with his pals around the desk) has repeated back to me:

"You want a ton of juice, like orange juice?" I've then gone on to say:

"No, sorry! I want a ton of wrath/anger". Right, that's better then.

Sometimes when a local Greek is talking I'll have a tad of trouble with his or her accent. There are several accents here on Rhodes and some of them are very, as we'd say in the UK, broad. I've told other friends, however, that "I can't understand what Periklis is saying, his offer is so strong."

The *piece de resistance* though is this one. There aren't many people who love Greece who aren't familiar with the most commonly used Greek swear word. Whereas in English one might say it's the "F" word, here in Greece it's the "M" word. The word '*malakia*' is understood to mean '*wanker*' and in some social circles it peppers conversations far too frequently. The thing is, there are two "M" swear words, one meaning '*wanker*' and the other 'a**hole' (*malaka*). Trouble is they're both related through etymology to another couple of completely acceptable adjectives. One means "soft" and the other "softener" as in fabric softener. In fact the inference behind the word 'soft' is what has led to the development of the word that means 'wanker' as referring to a man who's considered to be a bit 'soft' as in effeminate.

I was in company with a few families some time back and the conversation came around to shopping habits. Then it progressed to types of washing powder and related products (OK, so there were more women present than men at the time, honest). Right at the wrong moment (if you see what I mean) I decided to interject and show off my Greek by declaring that we bought a wanker in the supermarket for such and such a price, a bargain. Why all the shocked faces around me?

I don't think I need to explain further.

13. Capital

When I used to visit Greece in the early days, which was from 1977 onwards, my wife and I had the habit of staying with her relatives and basing ourselves there before disappearing off to the island of Poros for a couple of weeks or so. Her second cousin, Christina, and her family lived at the time in Kato Patisia, which back then was an OK suburb of Athens, but has in recent years become a lot less salubrious. Years before we actually moved out here to Rhodes cousin Christina had re-located to Politeia, Kifisia, which kind of reflected their changed fortunes as regards their economic situation. It's quite posh in Politeia. Kifisia is 'leafy suburb city', Potli Street in Katopatisia is 'block of flats-ville'.

When we moved here we had the idea that after a while we'd get back in touch with my wife's relatives in Athens and perhaps go visit them. Back in the first, probably ten years and more of our marriage we saw cousin Christina and her daughter Effi regularly, either in the UK or in Athens. As the years rolled on, however, contact became less and less frequent and eventually sadly ceased. It's not something we've ever been happy about, but it's the way of the modern world I suppose. The last occasion I can remember spending any quality time with them was when Christina, daughter Effi together with Effi's little toddling daughter came to visit us in South Wales at our modest little bungalow in Beddau, near Llantrisant. It must have been somewhere around the mid 1990's.

I have vivid memories of Athens from the many visits we made there when we were younger.

Despite all that the media thrusts at you, Athens is still an amazing place. OK, it has a very congested city centre area, packed with modern buildings and horrendous traffic. But it's not really all that big as cities go on a world scale. The population is about three and half million, so compared with London, which is nearer to eight and a half, you see what I mean. The Agora area right in the centre is truly amazing and abuts the areas known as Plaka and Monasteraki. The square at Monasteraki could be described as the spot where the ancient meets the modern. You can stroll down Mitropoleos from Omonia Square, a walk of maybe fifteen or twenty minutes, towering modern, faceless buildings rising up to your right and to your left, then suddenly there's a square before you, the opposite side of which is the imposing frontage of Monasteraki Metro Station. Looming large above and behind that is the instantly recognisable Athens Acropolis, with the Parthenon standing sentinel as it has done for thousands of years. One can't fail to be impressed at the sight.

To the left of the station is the old Byzantine church building that now houses the Museum of Greek Folk Art and from there you can either very quickly walk up the fascinating flea market of Pandrossou, or take Areos which brings you more directly to the Agora, the ancient Greek market place which is preserved as an open air museum. There you can wander two-thousand-year-old streets and examine the businesses and shrines that once graced this elegant city in the days when the Apostle Paul walked there. Above the Agora, spilling up the hillside of the mighty Acropolis is the Plaka, a maze of old streets and steeply stepped alleys, packed with shops and tavernas. Prior to 2014 we hadn't walked this area since 1982.

When we'd last emerged from the Metro Station at Monasteraki the traffic was able to pass to within a few metres of the building. Nowadays the entire square is pedestrianised, which is much better.

In 2014 we had an opportunity to pay a flying visit to Athens for three days only during July. Owing to the fact that we have work during the season, we couldn't stay any longer, much though we'd have liked to. We had mixed feeling about going. My wife had swallowed too much of the hype that led her to believe that perhaps it would be unsafe to walk the streets at night. TV reports of rising crime levels and violent clashes with the members of the 'Golden Dawn' so-called political party, footage of missile-throwing hooded youths and burning waste bins had all contributed to a feeling of unease on her part. When she was a teenager she spent successive summers there with her relatives, at a time when there was no such thing as graffiti, no major crime and virtually no crime against the person.

If one was to believe the media, Athens was becoming a war zone. What we discovered was that nothing could be further from the truth. Having secured a room at a hotel on Agiou Konstantinou, a straight, modern street running downhill from Omonia to Plateia Karaiskaki, we were going to be right in the centre of the modern city. Surely if things were as bad as the media made out, we were in for a rough ride.

I was eager to see how different my impressions were going to be from thirty years previously. We flew to Athens from Rhodes, and took the new Suburban Rail train into the city, where we then changed to the Metro for the final stage of the journey. The Suburban Rail trains are modern and fast, built only just over a decade ago for the 2004 Athens Olympics of course. The entire system, both Suburban and Metro works on trust. You buy your tickets and you head for the platform. There are machines that frank the tickets, but no turnstiles. You could theoretically travel anywhere for free if you were that kind of person. If a ticket inspector catches you, well, you take what's coming.

The idea is good, it's impressive. The vast majority of travellers do indeed pay for their tickets and the prices are reasonable. There's only one drawback. The beggars.

Almost every few minutes, once you've settled into your modern ergonomically-designed seat on the train and begun to take in the scenery, since the Suburban Rail network is overground, the first thing to hit you is more often than not the smell. Sometimes it'll be a diminutive woman with haggard, care-worn face and hardly any teeth left, carrying a baby on her hip. She'll trawl the aisle with a plastic cup wailing as she goes, desperately trying to extract some loose change from the paying passengers as she drags herself by. Other times it may be a really rough-looking man, probably only in his forties but looking sixty-plus. The smell on some of these poor unfortunates is on occasion so bad it makes you want to gag. We were travelling with a younger Greek couple. It was their first time ever away from Rhodes. They were figuratively clinging to us for dear life as we made the journey into the city. The two of them are very young, in their early twenties, and both were smartly dressed. In one instance a beggar leaned on the seat that the young wife was occupying, since she was beside the aisle. The man's stench was unbelievable and his grubby shirt was rubbing against our young friend's shoulder as he wailed a plea for some loose change.

I didn't know what to do for the best. Ought I to have tried to ease the man away physically? I have to admit that I was concerned about what his reaction might have been, not to mention the subsequent need I'd have had to wash my hands. In the end, he decided to proceed further along the train and we were left to await the next one. These trains have open aisles all the way through, thus enabling the beggars to make an approach to all the passengers in every carriage on board without hindrance.

You'd have to be extremely hard to not feel for these people, but if you were to help all of them you'd pretty soon be financially ruined yourself. You can't help but wonder how they got into this state, into this situation. Many of them seemed to us to be either Romany, or not Greek at all. It was very hard to tell though. We were pretty relieved to get off of the train in the end and reach the platform on the Metro to await the downtown link.

On the Metro the situation is not a lot different, although I'd say that there probably were fewer abject beggars and more ingenious buskers. There would be someone with a violin, with a little paper cup hanging by a string from the scroll end of the fingerboard. Some did something similar with a acoustic guitar. Some pulled little trolleys with a car battery on the bottom to power a tiny speaker system which pounded out some music or other while the owner would put on a dance show. There was even one ragged woman with long, lank black hair who evidently fancied herself as a great actor who'd arrive at your part of the carriage, carefully plan her entrance so that she had enough time between stations, then throw herself into a soliloquy from some Greek tragedy, reaching a crescendo that had you thinking, 'If this is a violent scene where someone stabs someone at the end, she may well act it out for real'. If you'd been wearing your iPod phones she'd still have drowned out your music for sure.

We'd come across something similar on the Paris Metro some years before. Somehow though, in Paris you got the sense that these people may have been students, enterprisingly supplementing their student income by doing a little busking on the side. Here in Athens though, there was an air of desperation about the whole thing. Throughout the journey from the airport to the Metro station at Omonia, where we left the train, climbed the steps to the street and walked the few hundred metres to our hotel dragging our wheeled cases behind us like recalcitrant children, I'd been observing our fellow passengers to see how they reacted to the beggars. Virtually without exception it seemed to me that all the Greek passengers reacted as though the beggars didn't exist. They sat or stood like statues until the nuisance moved away. One shouldn't be too hard on these commuters though. I found myself wondering how I'd handle such a situation if I were regularly travelling on these trains and thus meeting the same down and outs on a daily basis. A lot of regular folk may look prosperous, but in fact are without a doubt struggling themselves to make ends meet.

Once we were out in the 'fresh' air of a busy Athens street, our cases in tow as we walked to our hotel, our mood lightened somewhat. Here there were people, normal people if you like, to-ing and fro-ing, stopping at the periptero for a paper and a bottle of water, coming out of pastry shops clutching paper bags showing signs of the hot pies within beginning to stain the paper with the olive oil emanating from them. There were people sitting at tables under parasols sipping frappes and fiddling with their phones. No one seemed to be cowering in fear.

During our stay we wandered around the city every night. One night we found a gyros place down a side street from Omonia, where we ended up through circumstances being a party of around fifteen people, all Greeks save for me. We sat at tables all pushed together in the pedestrianised street and were served at table throughout, even though most of us only ordered souvlaki, maybe a couple of Greek salads. The staff were young, dressed trendily and very attentive. Pedestrians were passing both sides of our little knot of tables and this was from around 9.30pm until somewhere close to midnight. The atmosphere was informal, relaxed, holiday-like.

Following our very enjoyable period of *parea* we went to a bakery-cake shop right on Omonia itself and again sat at table to eat our *bougatsa*. Finally, at well after midnight me and the beloved and our two younger friends strolled the kilometre or so along a city centre street back to our hotel and retired for the night.

You know how when you're in a big city you often get a feel for the prevailing atmosphere around you? I used to live in Cardiff, in South Wales UK. Cardiff is a beautiful city, with some impressive civic buildings, a beautiful castle and a thriving nightlife. It's a great city for sightseeing with a population of just over 340,000, also quite small for a national capital and in fact a mere 10% of the population of Athens. We could go into the city during the evenings to attend a concert at the acoustically designed St. David's Hall, or the [as it was called then] Cardiff International Arena. We'd often go into town for a restaurant meal or a trip to the cinema or bowling alley. Yet we knew that there were certain streets that one would be wise to avoid. Even in the more relatively safe streets there were certain hours, like when the clubs were emptying, when you'd sense that apprehension in the air. Some of the back streets we'd never, never walk along after dark. Everywhere without exception, when the pavement cafés and restaurants closed they'd take all the tables and chairs inside before closing up. Roller shutters protected just about all the commercial premises. The telltale alarm boxes adorned every wall. Car theft was epidemic. I know, because I had a car stolen there. Statistically, you probably can't live in Cardiff for too long without suffering some kind of vehicle crime. I don't want to decry Cardiff. I still love going back there to visit. I'm just illustrating the point about sensing the atmosphere on the street. Multi-story carparks, great ugly edifices symptomatic of our times, were places where a person wouldn't want to enter alone during the late evening hours. Basically everything that could be vandalised or stolen had to be locked away every night.

When we walked the streets of downtown Athens maybe we were just lucky. Maybe we didn't go to the right (or perhaps 'wrong') areas. Yet to walk along a city centre street at 12.30am and pass not one, but every closed-up periptero and see newspapers and magazines still hanging all around the eaves secured with wooden clothes pegs, was an indicator of the social state of the city. To walk past café/bar after café/bar and see tables and chairs still in situ on the pavement, potted plants too, brought one a tremendous feeling of relief. The Athens I'd last walked in the early 1980s was still alive and well, at least most of it was.

The only appreciable, tangible difference, and it's a big difference it has to be said, is the prevalence of spray graffiti. In the 1980's graffiti was non-existent in Athens. I'd venture to suggest that it was virtually unknown in Greece as a whole. Nowadays, every blank wall, every roller blind, even every cast-iron rubbish bin, carries a huge array of ugly spray graffiti.

I blame the Americans. Not all of them of course (you have to be so careful, don't you). I'll explain.

When I first came to Greece the Greek entertainment industry fed the needs of the populace with and endless stream of innocuous movies starring Aliki Vougiouklaki and Dimitris Papamichael. Every movie was full of corny acting, with scenes that usually revolved around tavernas, kafeneions and quaysides and more often than not were crammed full of song and dance scenes, all of which involved *bouzoukia* and traditional Greek music. They seemed to celebrate a slightly unreal world where life for the average village Greek was exactly as one would imagine it to be in the movies. And of course, this <u>was</u> the movies. Real life never was like this, but it didn't matter. Now in 2017 you can still watch probably a dozen or so of such movies every week on Greek TV because it's a cheap way of filling the on-air schedule and money is tight.

Only from around the time when Greece entered the European Union did things begin to change and the more edgy, aggressive, violent, sexually-charged movies from the UK and America began to gain the upper hand to the extent that now, if you watch Greek terrestrial TV after 9.00pm, you'll see far more American TV series and movies (usually the ones that centre on major crimes, with accompanying realistic special effects, notably in the 'injury and mutilation' department) than you will Greek.

Of course young people have always been impressionable, but when their media brainwashing consisted of a bunch of Greek matelots dancing *Sirtaki* on the quayside, while the modestly dressed blushing young women of the local community looked on in admiration, then you could rightly expect the young to grow up doing nothing worse than smoking cigarettes over their frappé of a morning.

American and, to an extent, British, TV and movie output for the past two or three decades has been feeding Greek youths a different, more rebellious set of social mores and it shows. The graffiti on the New York subway trains for example has been seen in even fairly tame movies from as far back as the late eighties. It didn't take long for such a habit to catch on here in Greece once the entertainment exported from the USA and the UK reached the screens here. It's a sad fact which I suppose we can do very little about in this modern world, but due to the worldwide scope of the entertainment industry, American 'culture' is being imprinted on just about every other free country, for the better in some cases, for the worse in too many others.

I am in danger of digressing a little too far I know, but I'm sure you can see where I'm coming from. Returning to the Athens of today, graffiti aside, both my wife and I and our young friends walked the downtown streets without a feeling of foreboding very late into the night. As I said, you could argue that it depends where you go, but that's precisely the point really. If you're in Athens for pleasure, you're not really very likely to stray into the wrong areas anyway.

On the Saturday night of our stay we decided that it was an essential to eat out in the Plaka district. From our hotel's front door it was about a half-hour walk to Monasteraki, then up Areos, along Dexippou and after rounding a couple more corners we were in the thick of it. Plaka is vibrant, exciting and so attractive to the eye. Everywhere there are people strolling, examining menus, laughing in intimate groups over early evening drinks around bar tables under parasols, and traditional music wafts past your ears continually. The sound of laughter frequently regales your ears. If there is crime here you're not really very conscious of it. The tiny streets run this way and that, every corner revealing a flight of steps going either up or down that you feel you just have to investigate. All the way up or down these steps on either side, sometimes creating a zigzag path for those simply walking by, are tables and chairs perched on seemingly very dangerous edges of very old stone steps. The scene is a riot of colour and the atmosphere so infectious that you can't help but feel that, if only for this briefest of moments, all is right with the world. You want to sit at every taverna you walk past.

We eventually settled on a tiny table for two half-way up a steep flight of steps, where we could people-watch to our heart's content. There was a covered section in the taverna too, where a large contingent of mainly young tourists, evidently with their guide, from Canada we discovered later, was sitting, each and every member revealing how excited they were by the exuberance of their conversation. Our table sported a romantic little candle burning in a coloured glass cube, plus a single flower in a tiny vase. As the evening wore on and the sky darkened the atmosphere became even more dreamlike. I for one was wishing that I had a magic boomerang, remember that? I'd have thrown it again and again to make time slow down while I drank everything in. One of the most pleasing surprises about the prices for eating out in Plaka was that it's no more expensive than anywhere else. We ordered from a very personable waiter and didn't have to wait too long for our delicious meze of dishes.

There was an unexpected bonus to our evening too. The party of Canadians were evidently on an organised evening and there was entertainment laid on for their benefit. It wasn't long before a troupe of dancers was deftly manoeuvring between the tables while a few standing musicians played the accompaniment strumming on their traditional instruments. We had a ring-side seat and loved it. It was all I could do to restrain my better half from joining the dancers, but she was dancing with gusto from the waist up at the table anyway for most of the show. She's good at that, you should see her.

I had last been to Plaka in 1978, when my mother-in-law had guided us to a rooftop restaurant with a large terrace which had an uninterrupted view of the illuminated Parthenon above. For all I know it may have been the premises that her parents had occupied, since my wife's grandparents had a taverna in Plaka for many years leading up to World War Two. I never found out, but it didn't matter. We saw one of the best floorshows of traditional Greek entertainment that anyone could wish for and it has stayed with me for all the years since.

Athens still displays the same spirit that it did decades ago. Yes, there are problems, yes, there is graffiti which is a sad aspect of modern life one just has to live with, but as we walked back to Monasteraki in the small hours after a stupendous evening in an enchanted place, we were greeted by a huge crowd being entertained in the square by a modern rock band on a stage set to one side of the open space in front of the Metro Station. The mood was relaxed, the crowd was made up of all kinds of people, the band was a little like the Fleetwood Mac of the 1970s, with two girl singers out front, and they were rocking. It was quite a contrast to what we'd just enjoyed in Plaka, but every bit as enjoyable.

Greece is in crisis, it's true, but the indomitable spirit of these people and their dogged determination to carry on regardless in the face of the prospect of a very uncertain future is simply admirable. The Greek people know how to party and they know how to do it without getting drunk out of their skulls. The Greeks have the secret of great *'kefi'* and you'll still find it in spades in Athens.

14. The Spice of Life

Moving out here to a remote hillside rather than to a village was obviously going to mean less interaction with the neighbours than we'd been used to. Until the next two houses were constructed up the hill from us after we'd already been here for a few years, our nearest neighbours were Takis and his French wife Naomi, who live almost a kilometre down the valley, within a hundred metres or so of the road, the so-called *'kentriko dromo'*.

Apart from Takis and Naomi, our main points of contact with locals were going to be when we visited shops and businesses in the area, collecting our mail or perhaps while out walking.

Walking can be an interesting exercise if you choose to do it on a road where traffic will pass you frequently. To be honest, we usually only walk the "main road" in short bursts, while looking for other lanes or paths to take us elsewhere, like down toward the beach or further up into the hills above us. I say interesting because it doesn't take long for people who recognise you to begin at the least peeping their horns and waving as they pass, or, more likely, slowing down, lowering a window and offering a lift.

I know that walking is a dying pleasure everywhere these days, but here it's virtually already had a funeral. Now and again you may see a Bulgarian or an Albanian, usually female, walking to and from the nearest supermarket (Yes, I know, a rather ambitious epithet when you consider the actual size of the store being described) carrying two bulging shopping bags in either hand. This is usually because they probably can't afford a vehicle anyway or, if they can, it'll be a motor bike or scooter and their spouse will have used that to tootle off to work, if they're lucky enough to have any.

The only other person we see walking with any regularity is the Major, who lives down the valley from us, is probably around seventy, has a good head of white hair and daily goes for a constitutional with a stick which is usually waved from his right hand in a swishing motion as he strides along. There are a couple of ex-pats we have got to know who walk too, but they're not in our area, they're a little further away.

The upshot of this is that if someone you know sees you walking beside the road, they'll automatically assume that you'll be wanting a lift somewhere. When they pull over and say,

"Hop in, where are you going?" it doesn't compute when you reply,

"It's OK, we're walking on purpose. We like the exercise." You should see the look on their faces. *Kyria* Stamatia, the lady who owns one of the bakeries in Lardos village but isn't so often to be seen behind the counter these days owing to a bad heart, used to say to me:

"Gianni, a Greek would take his car to the toilet if he could."

I know what she meant. During the winter months we usually go out once a week to scavenge for wood for the log-burner. This winter (2016-17) has been our best ever in the fuel-for-the-fire department, since in the hills around the house we've discovered some new sources of well weathered pine that's ideal for chainsawing and stacking in our wood-store for immediate use. Some of this is as a result of the mini-tornado that tore up the valley a couple of years ago and rather obligingly ripped a few boughs off of some trees and deposited them within reach of a walker with a chainsaw.

In times past though we'd scour the beach for driftwood and then lug it home on our shoulders. Lots of locals now know us well enough, but in the beginning we were quite sure that they'd drive past tutting over how poor we must be to have to scavenge like that and then walk our burden home on foot. Well, I suppose all walking is done on foot really. There you are.

Something that you very quickly get used to here is the lack of precision when it comes to small change in the local stores. Even the tiniest of shops tends to be self service these days and you can often have a wander around, wedging yourself between overcrowded shelves either side of exceedingly narrow aisles, then turn up three feet away at the tameio [cash register] to find no one about. There may be a noise coming from a mysterious stock room through a doorway tucked behind a pile of cardboard boxes in the far corner of the room, or there may not be. More often than not the person manning (or woman-ing) the till will have gone over the road to the kafeneion for a coffee, or perhaps along to the bakery for a *spanakopita*.

It amuses me too how even the tiniest of stores has delusions of grandeur. The proprietor will have done his or her (OK, maybe 'their') level best to create an ambience like you'd find in the much bigger stores in or near the town. When you walk in there will of course be that little pile of plastic shopping baskets with retractable handles. Some stores even have half a dozen mini-supermarket trolleys that you'd be best advised not to take advantage of. You're extremely likely to get stuck somewhere on your way around the store while negotiating the sacks of potatoes on the floor, or maybe you'll collide with a display of special offers with tragic consequences. There will always be a mini-conveyor belt at the cash register and the proprietor will sit there trying to look like a supermarket checkout person when, if they were to stand up, they could probably reach the back wall of the store without leaving the checkout. Plus they only have the one till anyway. There's no room for two, leave alone a row of them. There will be those bouncy plastic 'shelf-talkers' touting special offers that are fixed to the front ledge of the shelves where the prices of the goods are displayed. They're OK in big stores where the aisles are wide enough, but in these tiny village ones they just brush your sleeve as you pass and then, because they catch, they'll spring out from their home and flutter to the floor. Then you're all embarrassed when you have to retrieve them. When you try slotting the thing back where it came from will the damn thing go in?

All that said, it is nice that when the person you need to give your money to finally puts in an appearance and the bill comes to, say €10.35, they'll more often than not say,

"Oh, give me ten."

There you'll be, riffling around in your purse for the small change and they'll be adding "*then peirazi*, it's no problem!"

Conversely, if the bill comes to €10.90, they'll often not bother to give you the ten cents change, but that's OK. When you add it all up you're definitely always up on the deal on a week-by-week basis.

You can also drop by the local café/bar and exchange a *kalimera* with your friend who waits the tables. They might say, "You having a drink?" and if you reply that you don't have any cash on you they'll say,

"Don't be silly. You can pay me whenever."

At our local coffee pit-stop I've lost count of how many times we've passed by while driving somewhere and collected a frappé to go and George has simply told me to put my money away. Of course he knows that I send anyone and everyone who's on holiday with us to see him for their drinks and maybe snack lunches so he's well happy to repay me in this small way.

The whole laid back way they deal with these things is a joy though. Thinking back to our old life I remember how precise everything had to be.

You had to be given the exact change, you had to make sure you paid the precise amount, even if the cashier was struggling for small change. No way could you leave without having resolved the issue to the penny, no matter if the cashier was your own mother. Even in these days when everyone's hypersensitive about having printed receipts here in Greece, the principle still applies. Close enough will do. They display a huge amount of trust with those whom they know. If you are waiting around at the till for a few minutes, they'll arrive safe in the knowledge that you wouldn't have dreamed of legging it without paying.

The culture is still one of honesty when it comes to personal property. OK, they may be a bit 'fly' when it comes to tax issues and that's a problem that needs addressing, but if you get up from a table at a café and walk off leaving your iPad behind, you can go back the next day and they will have kept it for you. Other customers will have handed it in, or even run after you to give it back. In the UK, sadly, you know that when you go back even after a mere five minutes it's much more likely that you'll never see it again. One time in London, my wife took her eye off her purse on a café table for about two seconds, while she rummaged in her handbag. There were people going and coming past the table continually and lots of people standing around and huddled around neighbouring tables too. When she reached out her hand to pick it up again, it wasn't there. That awful moment of disbelief overcomes you doesn't it. You break out in a cold sweat instantly. She stared at the table where she'd put it, then at all the faces around us. Not one person gave anything away yet the thief was more than likely staring back at her.

I'm not saying that it'll never happen here, but it's great deal more unlikely. I still sit in cafés here and marvel as I see Greeks with their wallets and mobile phones next to their coffee on the table in front of them, often not even glancing in that direction while they read the paper or carry on a conversation. I see people get up and go to the WC while leaving a phone on their table unattended. They come back knowing that it'll still be there.

Things are changing in Greece. I'd be wrong to say otherwise. But the fact is that here they're still a few decades behind western Europe and the USA in such things and it makes for a nicer, more relaxed and less stressful life.

I'm not a good sleeper. I've been a trainee insomniac now for a couple of decades and I reckon I'm due my diploma. This, though, has its upside. Almost every night, especially during the warm summer months, I find myself outside at 2.30am staring up at the night sky. The sky here is so, so different from the sky where we lived in the UK. Our last home there was in a small village, yet even along the pavements in our tiny cul-de-sac there were yellow sodium street lamps. Light pollution in the UK is lightyears worse than here where we live in Rhodes (see what I did there? Some of us have got it and some not, eh?).

I would say that in over fifty years living in the UK I may have seen a shooting star once or twice. Here I can see them several times a week. The night sky is truly awesome and you see so many more stars with the naked eye because if you live on a hillside a kilometre from the nearest road, the light pollution is zero. Living here I've learned to know the phases of the moon. I now know when it's waxing and when it's waning because here you can see it for the entire length of its cycle for most months of the year. The solar system which is our home is a truly astounding, immense clock and it's impeccably reliable.

My problem is that I'm usually only ready to sleep for a few hours come 3.30am in the morning. If for any reason I need to get up early and have to set my alarm, it'll usually go off when I'm in the middle of my best sleep time. I must be part-fruit bat.

My wife, on the other hand, leaps out of bed at the crack of dawn and is immediately ready for action. I confess I do occasionally have a 'normal' night when I'll sleep from perhaps eleven until seven in the morning, but as a rule it'll be more like I get up at midnight and return to bed at about 1.30am. I get up again at 2.15 and then go back to bed at 3.30am. That's when I finally feel myself drifting off like you do when you know that real sleep is on its way, and it's wonderful.

Next thing I'll know is I'll surface groggily and look at my bedside clock and see that it's 9.20am and the other side of the bed's not only empty it's stone cold. My dearly beloved will burst into the bedroom wth a nice cup of Earl Grey and a digestive biscuit for me, but this will only be after she's been out in the garden to clear up a few weeds and dead leaves from the rubber tree. In winter she'll have brought in some wood for the log-burner and hung out a line of washing, swept the kitchen floor, made the breakfast and solved the problem of world hunger. Maybe she'll have solved the refugee crisis too if it's half an hour later still.

When I was much younger I used to love getting up at the crack of dawn, which in summer would be well before six in the morning. Nowadays, because the owl in me is taking over, I'm beginning to forget that anything from 6.00am until 9.00am even exists. In springtime we have our part-time cat to look after too.

Mac and Jane, who live up the hill from us, have a gorgeous ginger tom (well, he was a tom once, wink, wink), named Simba. He wasn't always their cat. He moved here to our valley with his original 'owner' who lives in the house that was constructed up above theirs. But that owner adopted a few dogs and thus Simba moved house of his own accord. If you know cats you'll know what I mean. You never really own a cat, he or she deigns to live with you, right? Right.

Anyway, every March our closest neighbours head off to the UK for their grandson's birthday and the cat moves the fifty meters down the hillside to spend his vacation with us. Our garden is already his territory, so it's not too much of an upheaval. Give Simba a day or two and his feet are well and truly under our table. In fact, his whole body is because he likes nothing better than to curl up on one of our dining chairs (padded cushion, of course) under the table and to sleep there for a few hours.

We tend to have breakfast in March at the small round table just inside our

French windows, so we can eat while enjoying the view across the garden down the valley to the sea beyond that. The cat is Mr. Gregarious. He's always 'talking' and ceaselessly follows you around, especially if you're out in the garden. When we eat breakfast he's not happy unless we set a chair for him along with us. As long as he can curl up on his chair next to the two of us he's happy. Fuss him for a minute or two and he'll settle down contentedly while we eat. Once he's eaten his breakfast he's slightly more able to let us get on with things and he'll settle on one of the chairs near the window and, with his two front feet tucked under his chest, he'll gaze contentedly out the window, watching for birds.

The first time he did this and actually saw some sparrows he let out a noise that we at first didn't believe was coming from Simba. The flower bed across the tiles from just in front of the French windows is where we throw breadcrumbs for the sparrows to eat. We have to be careful when the cat's with us because if he's outside then the sparrows are in danger. I'm not knocking the poor guy, after all he's a cat. It's what they do. It's up to us to be sure that the birds are relatively safe.

One morning he was sat staring out into the garden when some sparrows landed, not three or four feet from the window, to begin pecking up the crumbs between the lantana bushes. Simba's ears went bolt upright and pointed toward the window as he lifted his head to "red alert" level and started letting out this mechanical, guttural sound from deep in his throat. When I was younger my family always had cats, for the first eighteen years of my life the house pet was a cat, yet I'd never heard a cat make this noise. I can't even rightly describe it here, except to say that if it had come from a small two-stroke lawnmower motor when someone was trying to start it up you'd not have batted an eyelid. From a cat however, cue manic laughter on our part.

They say animals have all kinds of facial expressions. If you'd seen Simba's face when we started laughing you'll know exactly how true that is. To say he was mortally insulted and not a little miffed would be an understatement. He knew well enough that the double glazing between him and some potential feathered prey was impediment enough, but it was as though he still couldn't let this moment pass without at least a comment to the effect that, give him free access to those birds and feathers would fly, not while still attached either.

We hadn't lived here for long when the hunters put in an appearance. Having lived where we did in the UK we'd never come into close quarters with anyone carrying a shotgun, ever. Here, every village is bristling with army-fatigue-clad, four-by-four-pickup-driving shotgun-toting hunters, who set out on evenings and weekends to drive up dirt tracks with their dogs on the back in ventilated boxes, or perhaps in a cage or box on a trailer bouncing along behind.

Walk the dirt tracks on the hillsides here and you come across spent cartridges every few metres. More often than not the hunters will simply drop the box in which they'd purchased their cartridges on the lane too as they stalk past. I love a lot of things about the Greek culture, but I'm not blind to their failings.

Greeks won't as a rule countenance buying second hand clothes for example, as it would betray a lack in their financial standing that would attract (in their view) sideways glances in the village. Probably has something to do with '*to mati*' as well. They are notoriously immune to any concern about the environment too in rural village communities. There are now TV ads these days about the need for recycling and of caring for the environment, but sadly such messages are in my opinion having more effect on urban dwellers than on the ageing population of remote villages. My wife and I walk the roadside verges all year round and the rubbish that accumulates there is far more often the result of Greeks chucking stuff out of car or truck windows than it is of tourists. In fact I'd say that the majority of tourists nowadays come from countries where recycling is the norm and care for the environment has a much higher profile.

The hunting season starts here during the third week of August and extends until the end of February. It would be easier to say when they can't hunt, since it's only the five months March through July and a couple of weeks into August. These months are the main breeding season and thus theoretically it ought to ensure that no species is placed under threat. Humans though, from what I've heard, maybe.

The most common prey is the chukar, a partridge with quite flamboyant plumage. Google it and you'll see what I mean. They're very similar in appearance to the red-legged partridge, although the latter is more commonly found further west in southern Europe (I love Wikipedia). The fallow deer on the island are not supposed to be hunted, but that's often ignored. We've seen the proof, sadly. Other prey include hares and rabbits and a few other small mammals. Birds of prey are illegal. Only what's classed as "game" is legal prey, but that's often ignored as we've subsequently learned.

"If it moves, they'll shoot at it." Someone told me once. The fact that the occasional hunter has been rushed to hospital with a slug of lead in his rear end bears witness to the truth of that statement.

When we first arrived here it was literally a couple of days after the hunting season began, a fact about which we were blissfully unaware. That was until Rambo appeared over the hillside in the area that's now part of our closest neighbours' garden, although back then it was just shrub-covered hillside. We'd been spending an afternoon busily getting our newly purchased sun loungers organised on the bare concrete screed that would eventually become our terrace (got to get your priorities right), when the peace was shattered by a couple of very loud bangs. Now, you may be the rural type who's always lived around shotguns, but little old us aren't in that category. We had to surmise that it was either a vehicle coming up the lane which was running on an exceedingly rich mixture and yet had an otherwise amazingly quiet engine, or perhaps the military were starting a manoeuvre rather too close to the house for comfort.

We walked to John and Wendy's end of the house, toward the direction from which the bangs had originated and there, trudging down from the ridge was this massive bloke in army fatigues with a smoking shotgun hanging from his arm. Now, to me, since I had little experience of such things, this was quite intimidating. Were they shooting (yeah, ha ha) a movie and I'd missed seeing the crew? The temperature was around 38°C and we were in shorts and tanktops. Here was this dark haired, bearded bloke, striding down the hillside in our direction looking to me as though he intended to blow my brains out, dressed in heavy military camouflage.

Hero that I am, I called my wife.

"Sweetie, since you speak the lingo, maybe you could ask him what he's up to?" This said of course with a sickly, ingratiating grin on my face. I did consider a career in politics once.

She didn't need to respond. Before either of us could dive for cover our 'guest' haled us with a wave and shouted a very friendly *"kalispera"*. Of course, he spoke passingly good English anyway and stood to chat for a while, learning with a few typically direct questions (another aspect of the Greek culture) about how we'd just arrived and that we were going to be living in this house *kalokairi-himona*, all year round (literally summer-winter). After welcoming us to the island he strode on into the undergrowth further down the valley, a couple of large dogs bounding after him, no doubt looking for stray Viet Cong.

We're used to it now. Going back, though, to that first encounter, it once again drove home to us the largesse of the Greek psyche. Foreigners are snapping up chunks of the Greek hillsides, land which has been used for sheep and goat grazing for time immemorial, land that the hunters have strode year in year out since they were knee high. Yet we come along, fence off a patch, throw up our little shangri la and expect to be welcomed.

And guess what, we are.

In chapter one of *"Moussaka to my Ears"* (volume two of the *"Ramblings From Rhodes"* series), I talked about Manoli and Felitsia, the goatherds that use this area to graze their herd. No sooner had we moved in than their herd was regularly trotting through what was eventually to become our garden. In the eighteen months or so before the perimeter fence was finally completed, we had goats staring through the French windows at us a few times per week. Some time before we had all of the fence completed, when it was perhaps 75% done, we chanced a few plants here and there and discovered that this unassuming couple were policing their animals to stop them eating our seedlings. More details in that chapter mentioned above.

Would I have done the same were I the goatherd and these foreigners had just seconded yet another chunk of my grazing land, land that had been used for such a purpose for time immemorial?

So anyway, the hunters display the same large-heartedness as the goatherds and simply work around us, although we need to remember who was here first when the occasional quiet afternoon or early evening has its peace shattered by the sound of shotguns. One needs to remember also, that for many of these men, it's a tradition that also goes back generations. They're not stalking the hillsides for sport, they're doing it to supplement the family table. I may not be a meat eater, but that doesn't give me the right to come over here and start waving placards at these folk.

Get yourself to virtually any village in the hinterland on a weekend morning and you'll see plenty of small groups of men, often just in groups of two or three, piling into pickup trucks with their firearms, loading their hunting dogs into their boxes on the back, always dressed in army fatigues, setting off for their field trips. Of course, I was wondering where they get the clothes from, since there don't appear to be army and navy stores here like you see in the UK. But with conscription still a fact of life for every young man in Greece, I assume that when they arrive home at the end of their term they have a few souvenirs that can be put to good use.

15. Health

Some years ago, while on holiday in Crete, we met a British couple who were living there. They were probably slightly older than us and, since we were at the time considering making the move, the subject of health care came up during the conversation. Turns out that the husband had needed a new hip, gone to the local doctor for an assessment and within a fortnight had been admitted to hospital, had the op and was back home recovering.

In the UK, as anyone living there will know, the National Health Service, which was started with such noble aims and ideals and has served the populace in a manner envied by the rest of the world for decades, is under immense pressure. There are simply too many patients and not enough resources. OK, one could address the issues of immigration and funding, but suffice it to say that when you need a new knee or a new hip, you're probably looking at a wait of some months, even over a year. The NHS web site states that for nonurgent operations there is a maximum waiting time of 18 weeks. That's four months. I think that a lot of UK residents, if asked if they waited that long would reply,

"I wish."

Here the system is slightly different. In the UK your GP will have to refer you to a hospital or specialist for the next stage. Here, quite often you choose your surgeon yourself. Aspects of the UK system would certainly improve the Greek one were they to be applied here, but the overriding factor here is that there is a much smaller population and far less demands are placed on local doctors' surgeries and hospitals.

Funding here is desperately low owing to the economic situation it's true. But the whole picture is far more complicated than that. Other factors make the playing field much more level than UK residents may imagine. I'm writing this chapter during March 2017 and, over breakfast this morning I was listening to BBC Radio 4 over the internet and the subject of the NHS once again was a hot potato. It seems that the hospital beds in the UK are over 90% occupied, which leads surgeons to put off non-emergency operations owing to the fact that there aren't the beds available for patients to recover on the ward before being sent home.

A few months ago there were reports on the UK TV news suggesting that the conditions in Greek hospitals were appalling, with patients lined up on gurneys in the corridors and some of them waiting for hours and hours to be seen while often experiencing pain and discomfort. This, of course is an awful scenario and one can only feel sorry for any patient and their relatives undergoing such an experience. The things is, and this is where I have to cautiously agree with someone I don't as a rule see eye to eye with, and that's Donald Trump, who for some inexplicable reason managed to get himself elected as the US president, when he refers to 'fake news'.

Having lived here now for something approaching twelve years, and having monitored the UK media during that time, especially since the Greek economic crisis had its cover blown by George Papandreou, I can only come to one conclusion. The UK media (and no doubt that of many other European countries) does indeed have more than its fair share of fake news.

I've banged on so often about this that anyone reading my stuff will be well aware of my view of the distorted picture that the media has painted of life here in Greece since 'austerity' kicked in. Nowhere is the point better illustrated than in the field of health and medical care. It's only a few weeks ago that I watched in horror as the BBC news in the UK showed footage of patients lined up in corridors in a major UK hospital, many of them experiencing inadequate care and attention while spending hours suffering the indignity of it all. Hold on a minute, didn't I just refer to the very same media, that is the BBC TV news (and not just the BBC, to be fair) carrying reports of how dire things were here in Greece where apparently the exact same conditions were prevailing? In fact, while I watched the footage of the UK hospital, which I think was in Blackburn, Lancashire, I had to blink a few times when I saw that the signs along the corridors were in English, not Greek. Yes, this was the UK, not Greece.

Pots and black kettles spring instantly and effortlessly to mind.

What's all the more galling about such misleading information is the fact that very recently the Theogenio anti-cancer hospital in Thessalonika was awarded first prize for the best presentation of a thoracoscopic surgery at an international competition held in Cincinnati, Ohio in the United States. Three years earlier, the same clinic was designated a "Centre of Excellence in Minimally Invasive Thoracic Surgery" on a European level. It also operates as an international training centre for thoracoscopic surgery. Greek hospitals in a morass of suffering and inefficiency? I don't think so.

Let me give you my own experience, since a few years ago I had to have my abdominal hernia fixed right here on Rhodes.

My hernia is a bit of a saga of a story really because, way back in the mists of time, about three months before I got married in fact, which would have been, ooh, before there was hair, I had one then too. It had sprung (right adjective there?) from the fact that I'd done a part time job for a while in a TV and radio shop in Bath called Ryland Huntley, at the bottom of Milsom Street and just two doors away from Carwardines, the delicious fresh coffee shop which used to roast its own blends of ground coffee on the premises. The smell of roasting coffee was perpetually tantalising everyone in the surrounding environs.

To have described working in Huntleys as torture, when I was unpacking TV sets and lovingly dusting B&O hi-fi systems that I'd never be able to afford myself, whilst being perpetually tormented by that delicious coffee aroma drifting along the street would be putting it mildly. See, back in those days it was the TV sets that were huge, with great big pregnant backs and very heavy cathode ray tubes inside them, whilst more men were slim and lithe owing to their doing a lot more physical graft. These days of course, it's the other way round. TVs are wafer thin and most couch potato blokes have the huge bellies, eh?

So, anyway, after a few months of precariously climbing very high step ladders, carrying huge cardboard boxes which contained fat cathode-ray-tube TV sets so that I could stack them on top of a dozen other boxes of similar size, I knew I had something wrong down below. A visit to the GP confirmed that I had myself a hernia on the right side and this was going to need surgery.

Well, here I was now 40 years later with a similar problem, only on the other side, so early in November it was off to the local doctor's surgery in Gennadi to see what the doc would say. Now, the system out here is quite different from the way things are done in the UK. In the UK the GP will assess the situation and, having decided that you need to go to hospital, refer you, right? I mean, you'll go home and wait for the letter summoning you to attend at such and such a date. Here it's much more laid back. I'll explain.

There I was dropping my trousers just far enough for this young doctor (who looked to me like he'd just put his Lego bricks down, he was *that* young) to have a gander and then he says,

"Hmm, yes. It had better be sorted out. Do you have a surgeon in mind?"

I kid you not. I really felt like saying,

"Oh yes, of course. I'm on first name terms with <u>all</u> the staff at the Rhodes General Hospital. We're always hobnobbing over a Metaxa or two, don't you know!"

What I actually said was, "Well, no."

The Doc replied that there were several surgeons in Rhodes who carry out such procedures, and I'd be better deciding myself which one to approach. He then looked at me questioningly once again. In a blinding flash I suddenly thought of my businessman friend Stelios in Rhodes Town, someone who regularly visits sick friends in the hospital and does know a lot of people there. He's that kind of guy.

"Shall I call my friend?" I asked the child across the desk, to which he said, "Yes, sure."

So, you can picture the scene. Here I was sitting in the local surgery calling my friend on my mobile phone. He answered and asked me how I was, how was Maria, what was the weather like down our way and the like. I replied affably and then cut to the chase.

"Stelio," I began, "Can you recommend a surgeon to operate on my hernia by any chance?"

Stelios replied, "Well, there's so and so, and then there's also..." whereupon I interrupted and suggested that he talk directly to the GP across the desk from me. So now, I was feeling that all this is very surreal as I ended up sitting and waiting while the GP chatted to my friend on <u>my</u> mobile phone, saying things like "Yea, OK. Well he'd be a good one, 'cos he knows me. You have his mobile number by any chance?" ...and so on.

The upshot was that a surgeon was agreed upon and I was given his mobile phone number and told that <u>I'd</u> need to call him to arrange an initial examination at the hospital, before being booked in for the operation. Now I don't know about you, but I felt a bit nervous about cold-calling a surgeon. Why?

1: The bloke who'd done my other side way back in Bath, UK in the middle ages was the kind of man who wore half-glasses and struck fear in the poor mortals whom he deigned to help with his scalpel. I had vivid memories of him sitting on the end of my bed after I'd been "done" and feeling like I was in the presence of greatness, what with his high forehead and greying temples and stuff. After all, I was only about twenty and he was probably 60-ish.

2: What if I called the bloke just as he was inserting a scalpel into some other patient in theatre? I wouldn't want to be responsible for some other poor soul getting a bigger and more untidy scar than he or she deserved, always assuming that the shock of the phone ringing didn't lead to some inner organ being punctured or anything like that!

So, I decided to text him. I know, …weird isn't it. I <u>texted</u> a surgeon I'd never met before to tell him that he'd been selected to sort out my hernia. Mind you, I came up trumps I think. The bloke called me back right away (evidently not in theatre then. That is of course, unless he was holding someone's carotid between his thumb and forefinger and telling his assistants around the operating table, "I'll just get this"!) and he was friendliness itself. We arranged a time of mutual convenience and I duly drove up to the hospital one Saturday morning.

What is very good here is that you don't wait for months to get your op done. Whilst I was with him in his office, the surgeon had flipped open his appointment book (nothing as advanced as a computer diary in sight) and apologised that I'd have to wait a couple of weeks, which was owing to the fact that he'd be nipping off to a conference in Berlin that coming week, then operating in a hospital in Crete before returning to Rhodes. But, I was booked to check into my hospital bed three weeks Monday, for the operation to take place on the Tuesday. I'd be going home on either the Wednesday or Thursday. That was, of course, as long as some other bloke with a hernia didn't call the surgeon just as he was inserting his scalpel into my abdomen, thus causing me major injury or loss of life.

I don't suppose the easiest of circumstances in which to strike up a casual conversation with someone is at the time when they're dragging a Bic razor (sorry about the advertising) all over your privates.

"Off anywhere nice for your holidays next year?" doesn't seem the appropriate thing to say when you're flat on your back and naked from the chest to the knees, then you look down and see this bloke, all in green 'scrubs', lifting certain parts of your family allowance out of the way in order to make sure he doesn't miss a bit.

There's something that makes one feel deeply vulnerable when one's pubes are all gone and you look down at the area around your nether regions and it looks like a chicken just about to go into the oven. Having at the time still sported my hernia, the resemblance to the unfortunate bird was even more striking. I found myself wondering, 'Does this bloke spend all day shaving people before surgery, or are there other aspects to his daily grind that make his life a little more worthwhile? What does he talk about when he's propping up the bar of an evening with his mates? Does he have a scale of 1-10 by which he measures the blokes he's shorn? "Tell you what Kosta, you'd have been dead jealous of this bloke I did this afternoon…"'

Anyway, here I was in Rhodes General Hospital, "Andreas Papandreou Hospital" to give it its full and grandiose title, for my hernia operation. I now can speak from considerable experience and can possibly put a few readers' minds at ease, should any of you out there ever find yourselves in need of treatment over here on Rhodes.

For starters, like I said, I was amazed at how soon I was booked into the system to get my op done. There I was at the ridiculously early hour of 8.00am on Monday, November 25th, checking in at the patient reception desk at the hospital. Paperwork out of the way and a wad of stapled-together

A4 photocopies now in hand, followed by my trusty wife (laden down like a beast of burden) I made my way to the fourth floor, B Surgery Unit.

Why was my better half laden down as described above? Well, the Greek system has always been a little different from that in the UK. It has nothing to do with austerity or anything like that. It's merely the fact that here in Greece the culture is that a hospital patient usually has someone from their family at their bedside for the duration of their stay, you know, someone to find and put on your slippers for you; put them on your feet of course, not theirs. If they put them on their own feet you'd be seriously thinking about whether you made the right choice of hospital carer in the first place. This is due to the fact that the Greek health system never has spent money on some of the little extras that we expect in a UK hospital. All the staff that do look after you are professionals and extremely good at their jobs, let's get that out of the way first. But they don't employ as many ancillary staff as in the UK and they don't always provide stuff like a jug of water at the bedside, that extra cup of tea half-way through the afternoon and so on.

So, my wife, ever the pragmatist, decided to come prepared for all eventualities. I had with me a rucksack containing my toiletries, tracksuit bottoms and a t-shirt for my stay (haven't had a set of pyjamas since I was about eleven) and my slippers. She, on the other hand, conscious of the fact that she'd be "camping" by my bedside for the three days or so of my stay, carried a pillow, replete with fresh pillowslip, a bag of mixed nuts and raisins, some crisps and savouries to nibble, a couple of bottles of squash, a vacuum flask, a bottle of water and a toiletries bag stuffed with all her creams and stuff. Oh, and a full-sized bath towel plus one of those 'scrunchy' things you use in the shower to lather up the shower gel, yes she brought some of that along too. Then there was a bag of fruit (bananas, apples etc.) and a wind-up torch in case of there being no power during the nights. I thought she was being a little mega-cautious there, but she brought it anyway. Nearly forgot, she also had in a bag with her a few changes of underwear, whereas I'd brought one spare pair of briefs, which I only ended up changing into on the morning of our departure.

I couldn't talk her out of bringing that torch. The fact that there had to be a generator back-up system at the hospital in case of power cuts didn't sway her. Imagine though, a hospital in Greece without a generator. Not many patients on constant monitoring in Intensive Care with all those machines that beep and stuff would survive if they simply let the whole place lapse into darkness when the power went down. Imagine too, being in theatre under that huge lamp above the operating table when everything gets plunged into darkness. Nah, there had to be a generator. There did, didn't there?

When we rolled up to the Staff desk on the ward I swear they looked at her and thought she'd just come out from under a railway arch. Mind you, since there aren't any railways on Rhodes, perhaps not, but you get the picture.

I was soon signed into the ward and a very nice receptionist took us along to our room, which consisted of four beds, an ensuite and a fabulous view.

There was even a wardrobe near the door for each patient to cram into all the stuff they wouldn't need until it was time to check out and go home. There was the usual bedside cupboard and shelf, in fact, the whole place looked exactly like you'd expect of any modern hospital ward room. Mine was the bed furthest away on the right, beside the window, from which we had a view across to Turkey and Symi, plus of the coast at Ialyssos and we could see the northern end of the airport runway at Diagoras. Had it not been for the fact that I was in for surgery, it would have made a very acceptable hotel room. I reckon the view was a lot better that quite a lot of hotel rooms on the island anyway.

There then began the round of things that they need to do before you get "surgerized". First, I had to go for a blood test. Young chap in blue scrubs, busily chatting to his mate in similar attire about football, soon got that out of the way. Well, actually it was his second attempt to find a vein that would surrender some of my blood which succeeded. I'm with Tony Hancock on that one. I'm sure my body doesn't want to let any of its component parts go without putting up some resistance. It's understandable.

Then it was back to the ward to sit on the bed and wait. An hour or more passed by and then I was told, "off you go to get your chest X-rayed". Got to see if anything would affect you going under the anaesthetic. Nice little jaunt down to the ground floor, where I handed in my bit of paper along with the rest of the waiting inmates and I was soon called in by a businesslike woman who told me to stand in front of one of those unwelcoming cold panels. I was immediately put in mind of those newsreel clips about women going for mammograms. I had my hands thrown around each side of the panel and my chest pressed up against it. Before I could say "cold nipples!" she told me it was all done and I could return to the ward.

The day drifted by as we watched the weather close in ever more.

We were very pleased to find that my next door patient, a very nice bloke called Theophilos, was extremely amenable, as was his wife Soula. There were no patients in the other two beds, something which was to prove most useful. Chatting together helped to pass the time and eventually, some time around dusk, I was told to go and have my interview with the anaesthetist. Theo would be going down for his surgery (same problem as me) on the afternoon of the day before me. So I was rather keen to see what kind of state he'd be in when they brought him back, since it would have a bearing on what I could expect.

The anaesthetist was very nice, as was everyone I'd so far encountered. He told me that I could elect to have local or general. Local?! For a hernia?? I told him I was well and truly intent on being asleep for the duration thank you very much. Imagine actually hearing what's going on!! No way José. No, I was going to be on fluffy clouds in faraway places if I had anything to do with it.

Next was my turn to be shaved, hence the scene described a little earlier. After the bloke had completed his work and stood back to admire his accuracy and the cleanness of the whole thing, he hit me with: "Now, if you'd just turn on to your side, I have to give you an enema. This won't hurt…" Resisting the urge to say "I hardly know you!" or , "Ooh, Matron!!" I did as requested. No further comments necessary about this bit.

My last "appointment" of the day was a final interview with the surgeon himself. I entered the examination room where he said,

"Hello John. Everything OK? Drop your trousers, let's have a look." It's only people of a few very specific professions that can say things like that when you think about it. He told me to remain standing as I exposed the offending bulge.

"*Poh Poh!*" He rather helpfully exclaimed, "*einai mega'li!!!* [it IS big!]". I have to say that he was right. To be honest, if I'd told you that I'd swallowed a tennis ball and it had migrated to the area of my lower left groin, you'd have believed me. Anyway, he then sat me down and ran through the results of all the tests I'd had done that day. The blood had revealed no problems with diabetes, no kidney problems, in fact everything was hunky dory. In fact [and this is where I have to boast, folks, with all humility…] he clipped my chest x-ray on to the light box above our chairs and raved about how clear it was. "Like an 18 year old!!" He exclaimed. "Totally clear. Perfect!" You can allow yourself a slight feeling of exhilaration when you hear that at 60 years of age. See, there's a plus point to such an experience. You get a free MOT test thrown in (For our non-UK friends, that's the UK annual roadworthiness test for vehicles over three years old).

By the middle of the evening I'd sampled the hospital food a couple of times. They allowed me to eat up until the evening and to drink water up until midnight. After that it was "nil by mouth" until after the op. The food is very acceptable. No, it's not Cordon Bleu, but it fills a hole and I certainly wasn't so averse to it that I'd have wanted to complain. They'd been told when I checked in that I was vegetarian and they gave me a pasta and cheese dish for supper on Monday evening, accompanied by a small side dish of Greek salad. There was yogurt and chopped fruit for dessert and a nice brown bread roll too. If I had any complaints at all it would have been that I'd have liked more salt. But that may well have had something to do with the fact that I was in a hospital anyway. In fact, the paper napkins that came with the food were emblazoned with the "Omorfos" logo. Omorfos is the very company run by my friend Vaso, the young lady who provided the lunches on the lazy day cruises that I'd worked on all summer once for Thomson (TUI). Small world. If you go into hospital out here, take a salt cellar with you, job done.

As I said, Theo was 'done' the evening before me. They brought him back to the ward about two hours after he'd gone down. He was wide awake and chatting with the porter who was wheeling him along. Good sign then. The op itself only takes about half an hour, and his wife had followed his bed down with him and came back with him too. At this stage we didn't know whether she'd been allowed in to watch the whole thing, but rather expected not. There was no sign of her having eaten popcorn.

Next morning at six o'clock sharp the lights went on and a loud woman's voice announced that they were going to change Theo's drip (Ringers Lactate I think, to re-hydrate and take away hunger pangs while one recovers from the anaesthetic). That's something that seems to be common to hospitals the world over. No one, but no one gets to sleep on past 6.00am.

Three hours later and me now dressed resplendently in that paper gown thing that's all open at the back, along with some knee-length stockings that are meant to help with the circulation while you're out for the count, the lady porter arrived to wheel me down for my surgery. My wife had an anxiety attack, then quickly recovered and followed the bed as I began the trip down two floors to the theatre. As I was being wheeled along the corridors everyone I passed looked my way and said "*Kali epitikia*", which means something like, "good luck". To be strictly accurate, it translates as "good success". Not sure quite how to interpret that sentiment though.

Once out of the elevator (OK, "lift") we arrived at the swing doors leading into the surgery area and the porter told my wife that it's thus far and no further. She could wait just over there, where there were a few chairs and a couple of other people looking anxious. Once through the doors I was struck by how all the decor was now brilliant white, whereas elsewhere it had a kind of cream motif. Before a few seconds had passed and a few medical staff had done likewise, all looking like they're on a mission, I was wheeled into a side room, where a bloke in the ubiquitous green "scrubs" was waiting for me. He wheeled a stainless steel operating table covered in a spotless paper sheet alongside my bed, stretched a green sheet over me and bade me take hold of the top corners of it. Once I have done that, he, quick as a flash, reached under it and whipped away my bedclothes. Then he helped me transfer myself on to the operating table, which he then wheeled a few metres further into the theatre itself. I found myself saying to him, as much for my own comfort as anything else,

"It's like a factory isn't it. A constant stream of bodies coming in this door and out that one."

He replied, "Yes. Actually, we often say we're like bakers, shoving trays into the oven and pulling them out when they're done!" I was now a figurative loaf folks.

Once I was in the theatre it all happened very fast. The anaesthetist I'd had the interview with the day before was there and soon began preparing to administer the anaesthetic. Next thing I knew, I was coming round and the surgeon himself was speaking to me.

"All fine John. You're done, Everything went well."

There was a woman's voice to my right. I turned my head and there, not more than a metre from me, lay a young woman, evidently waiting to go in from where I'd just come out. She was pretty wound up, not settling to this whole experience very well. I found myself, still woozy, saying to her,

"Don't worry love. It's all going to be fine. there's nothing to it." Before I realised what was happening, some member of the surgical team pulled back the white sheet covering her body and she was starkers, but evidently very pregnant. I assumed she was in for a Caesarian. Either that or it was their way of <u>really</u> waking you up! I had the presence of mind to look the other way and fortunately was instantly on the move again.

They keep you in there until you come around properly. Before long, though, I was back in my own bed being wheeled out through the double doors, where my wife instantly arrived at my side. I'd been in there all told about two hours. She later told me that she'd been comforting a bloke whose wife was in there giving birth. I think I may have met her.

Back in the ward I was vaguely aware that there was a drip in my left hand, through a catheter. It had two stop-valves, through which they, over the next 24 hours or so, administered the Ringer's Lactate, some antibiotics and some pain killers. For most of the rest of the day (Tuesday) I slept, woke up, sipped water, then slept again, feeling to be honest, extremely comfortable and protected, which indeed I was.

There was a substantial team of nurses and whatever else you'd call them, constantly coming and going, checking my pulse, taking my blood pressure, administering my drips, and every one of them kindness and professionalism itself.

Of course, once you're over the op, it's mainly downhill from there on. So I'd be up at the window gazing at the view and watching as the weather improved.

All in all, when we finally "checked out" we almost felt quite sad. We'd only found out on the last evening that one can rent a telly [digital service] for € 3 a day, so we did watch "*Kati Psinetai*" ["Something's Cooking", or in the UK, "Come Dine With Me"] once. I thanked all the staff, the whole team on the ward, as I signed out at the desk and I was quite looking forward to seeing them again on the following Wednesday when I was to go in to have the stitches taken out, which, incidentally, was done by the surgeon himself, not some junior medical staff member.

The whole experience from beginning to end left me feeling deeply grateful to have been looked after so well by such kind and professional people who worked their socks off, much like medical staff the world over, it seems. On talking to Greek friends about how it all went, one female friend said,

"Yes, well, you would get treated like that, you're a *xenos* [foreigner]. It's not the same for us Greeks."

I have to say that I don't agree with her. After all, in the bed next to mine there had been a Greek man, Theo, and he'd been through exactly the same procedure and received the exact same treatment. Plus in the other rooms along the ward there were Greeks, one from another island, Kos, all of whom were done in the same two-day session. It seemed to me that I was the only foreigner among a list of Greeks and we all received the same care.

Interestingly, I placed the bulk of this story on my blog in two successive posts. I received more feedback on this whole story than on probably the previous four or five put together. Most of the feedback was from UK resident men who told me that they'd had their abdominal hernias done in their local hospital and after reading my tale they'd wished they'd been 'done' out here on Rhodes. Without exception they said that they'd been sent home the same day that they'd had the operation. OK, so one likes to be in one's own home, but with a brand new wound and a possible need for care in case of infection? Doesn't do much for your confidence in the system. I remembered my previous experience back in the 1970's and the fact that the surgeon, I remember now, he was called Mr. Schofield, had told me that I was not under any circumstances to sneeze for a couple of weeks after the op. This would carry the very high probability of opening up the wound again. Coughing too was to be avoided if at all possible. I have a vivid recollection of walking along my hallway at home (and back then they did keep you in for a couple of days anyway) and stopping, ramming my fist into my abdomen in preparation and letting out a huge ah-TISH-HOO! For a few moments I was petrified, but fortunately there was no harm done.

Nowadays, in the UK they'll say, 'Oh yes well, care at home is much better for the patient's peace of mind and comfort'. Crap. They need the beds, pure and simple, as evidenced by the TV news reports I refer to at the top of this chapter.

Of course I could go into all the problems with material and drug supplies that the Greek health service undoubtedly is experiencing. This, though, does not translate into a lack of care at the bedside.

I'll tell you something else too. The floor on my ward was well worn. Yes, like in all hospitals it's composed of that vinyl-looking stuff that curls upwards at the skirting board to make cleaning easier and prevent corners where dirt can build up. Hygiene after all is paramount in a hospital. If there were no budget constraints I'm quite sure that the floor on my ward would have been replaced by now.

Tell you what, though. It was spotless.

Every day a young woman (yup, she was Albanian) would come in and mop the floor, then wipe it clean. I'd have eaten my dinner off it without hesitation. I can speak from experience when I talk about the ward floors in the UK. Both of my parents, even though they lived pretty active and full lives until they died, were occasionally in and out of hospital during the last decade or so of their respective lives. I've lost count of how many hospital visits I made to see one or the other of them. I also remember vividly the dust and hair balls rolling around on the floor under their beds. There are those in the UK National Health Service who bemoan the demise of the ward matron. I reckon I sympathise. The introduction of private contractors too is a bone of contention. I don't want to get political here, but I am making relevant observations.

So, in conclusion. Don't believe everything you read in the papers. And take a huge dose of scepticality before watching the 'fake news' on your TV. That's my verdict and I'm 'on the ground' here in Greece as it were.

16. Health 2

Here in Greece there are local medical centres, what we'd call doctors' surgeries in the UK, operating in much the same way as they do in Britain. The big difference is how long it takes to get seen by a GP. Once again, without wishing to express a political opinion, I can state with confidence that probably the majority of people in the UK aren't at all happy nowadays with the way it all works, or doesn't work.

I'm old enough to still remember the days when your local surgery was staffed by only one, two or at the most three GPs, and you had your own family doctor who knew you by name and would be able to ask you with confidence how your granny was doing and you'd know that he actually knew her personally and hadn't just consulted a few notes before letting you into his office. I reckon when I was small our doctor even knew our cat's name.

Perhaps it's asking too much to go back to the days when your local GP would make house calls if you were unwell. These days, so I hear, you'd have to be at death's door to get a GP to come to the house, and even then holding it open with your foot. It takes so long to get an appointment that you're more than likely to be over the problem before you get to see a doctor anyway, right? Some years before I left the UK I had a rather unpleasant encounter with a GP at the practice near our home at the time in Fairwater Green, Cardiff, Wales. In fact, I'm probably talking the 1980s here and it's become much worse since. Anyway, I'll tell you what happened.

Bear in mind here that both my wife and I have always been in pretty good health and never ones to bother a doctor unless there was a pretty good reason. OK, I get it when some doctors tire of the time wasters, those who want to see a doctor for every little sniffle. These are possibly lonely folk who don't have much going on in their lives and so to arrange a visit to the doctor is a little highlight. Such people I do feel for, but it doesn't make the doctor's life any easier. I would assume though that a good GP would be well aware that if a relative stranger walks into his or her office one day then there would in this case probably be a pretty valid reason for the visit.

I seem to recall that I had some kind of problem with my calf muscle and it wouldn't go away. Back then I was under a lot of pressure and was suffering from stress too. In fact I eventually ended up at the hospital having an endoscopy to see whether there was an ulcer lurking down there somewhere. But backtracking a little, I'd been advised about which doctor to try and see by a friend who knew the GPs well in our local surgery, whereas I had no idea because I tended to go see a doctor every ten years or so. The problem was, to get an appointment with the lady doctor I'd been advised to see was a near impossibility owing to how popular she was. So I had to accept the GP that was available. That in itself ought to have rung the alarm bells. One does wonder sometimes why people with a certain personality ever become doctors, which is a caring profession, right? One also gets doubts when one has to settle for the GP no one wants to see.

So, there I was, sitting in the waiting room for my 4.00pm appointment, which I'd booked a week in advance (to see the doctor I'd been advised to see would have meant waiting a fortnight or longer). I eventually got in at half past four and sat down at the doctor's bidding.

"Now, what can I do for you?" Asked the medical man.

"Well, Doctor," I began, expecting as one does, a sympathetic ear, "There are two things really…"

Before I could say anything more, he interrupted me with…

"Well, you'd better decide which is the more urgent because you only have ten minutes."

Like I said, why do people with certain personalities become doctors? This bloke knew that I wasn't a time waster, yet this was his opening gambit. When I asked why I only had ten minutes, he replied:

"Otherwise you need to book two appointments in succession."

Yea, I was sure to have known that wasn't I.

Here, the local health centre is in Gennadi village, four kilometres down the road from our house. If you need to go to the doctor's, you simply call in when the surgery is open, which it is daily from around 8.30am. There may be a couple of old *papous* or *Yiayias* in there, perhaps a woman with a sniffly child, but you'll be ushered in to see the doctor probably well within half an hour. No appointment, no waiting for a couple of weeks.

When I first went there about my hernia I didn't know doctor Niko. He it was whom I described as like a child in the previous chapter. Not that I go there very often, but for reasons that shall become known in the remainder of this chapter, I now know him better and he's probably in his late thirties. He does have a wife and young family so I've recently learned. Bet they don't see all that much of him.

You know how in the UK we so often say, 'You know you're getting old when Policemen start looking like schoolchildren'? I'd say we could add doctors to that too. That's it then. I must be reaching that stage where 'the summer's almost gone, the winter's tuning up' as Leonard Cohen once sang. He also sang, in the same song, 'And I can't forget, I can't forget, I can't forget but I don't remember what."

Where was I? What was I going on about? Oh, yes, the doctor's surgery in Gennadi. There is a small but dedicated staff working there. I don't know them all that well, since as I said earlier, I'm not a regular visitor to the doctor's surgery. Yet a couple of years ago a friend out here who runs a bar in Lindos ran a charity event to raise money for their own local health centre. They held a bring and buy/coffee morning and with the proceeds were able to purchase much-needed supplies for the doctor and his team. Not long afterwards I was chatting to a couple of fellow ex-pats who live not far from me over a drink at the Gré Café here in Kiotari. Pete and Maggie are the kind who'll always turn up for a fundraiser, bless 'em. Pete mentioned this "Help for Health Lindos" event, which incidentally also contributed to the Arhangelos Health Centre from their proceeds too, and suggested that it may have been nice if they'd sent some of the proceeds to our own local surgery in Gennadi.

I grasped the nettle, got the bit between my teeth, took it on board and ran with a germ of an idea. I soon found out that running a charity event is anything but straightforward. In fact it's fraught with pitfalls and dangers. For instance, if you decide to hold it in a bar, there are all kinds of local authority restrictions that apply and forms that need to be filled in. This will inevitably involve visits to the local *Dimos* and probably too the Police Station, not to mention one's own accountant. The whole event may be run by volunteers for a noble cause, yet chances are the government will want to slap a hefty tax on all monies accrued. Yuk. Visions of all these potential visits soon had me thinking, 'forget it'.

Then I talked it over with Melanie, who ran the Lindos event at her bar.

She was very helpful and told me that if you hold the event in someone's garden and no one advertises fixed prices for the goods they bring to sell for the cause, you can probably get away with it without interference. It'll be simply a bunch of friends gathering to collect a bit of cash. Aha, there was the way forward then.

It is true that, regardless of all the positives I referred to in the previous chapter, the economic hardships are making it extremely difficult for local surgeries to function. They don't have the money even for daft things like pens, toilet rolls, paper clips, medical dressings or prescription pads, paper hand-towels and so on. The Gennadi Health Centre serves a huge catchment area taking in villages like Apolakkia, Messanangros, Arnitha, Vati, Lahania, Kattavia, Asklipio and more besides. In short, an awful lot of people's health and wellbeing would be under threat were it to close. And there have been rumours on and off over the past few years. There are a few philanthropists in the area who have been like a lifeline it's true. One of these is the owner of a chain of hotels, whose family comes from the nearby village of Asklipio. He has continued without letup to supply funds from his own pocket to help sustain the service that Dr. Nikos and his tiny team provide.

I was horrified, though, on talking with those 'in the know' to hear that running an event like a bring-and-buy entirely with volunteers and for a worthy cause, runs the risk of tax inspectors turning up and dipping their fingers into the pot and walking off with a third of what you've taken.

After having weighed it all up though, and after also having been assured by Julia, a local Englishwoman who's used her house for such events on numerous occasions (often for animal charities) over the years, that we could hold it at her house, which has a good sized garden, I thought, 'stuff it, I'm going to do it.'

I started a Facebook page and we fixed a date in early 2016 to run the thing. People turned up with local handmade crafts to sell plus a cornucopia of second hand stuff too numerous to mention. We were overwhelmed with stuff to be offered as prizes in a 'raffle' or, as I preferred to call it, a 'draw'. Julia's dining table was brimming with bottles of wine, jars of preserves, toiletries, local craft items and more. I called it a 'draw' because, once again, one has to be very circumspect when it comes to what the authorities may construe as running a gambling operation that would once again incur paperwork, a licence, possible prison sentence etc..

Instead of using a pre-printed roll of numbered tickets, I spent ages at home the evening before the event cutting up A4 pieces of paper into small squares about two inches along each side. I bound a block of them with an elastic band and then made a sign telling people to write their name on one of the pieces (with the pen I provided), fold it and drop it into the straw fedora that I supplied for the very purpose. It worked very well. I drew the pieces of paper out of the hat at 12 noon and soon became hoarse with shouting out names above the general hubbub. All in all the whole thing went well and a solid number of ex-pat British turned out to support us, plus a few local Albanians from the village.

What was a real success though was the fact that a local businessman, Dimitris, turned up and made comments along the lines of,

"You folk are doing a good thing. I wish that we Greeks would take this to heart and do likewise."

Dimitris is quite a young man with a young family. He has recently taken over ownership of a small studio-hotel in Gennadi village. The hotel had been closed for a few seasons, lending a tired, abandoned feel to that area. Tourism has never been high level here, but it did have a kind of heyday a couple of decades ago. The village has a good enough clutch of decent tavernas and bars, plus several lovely tavernas right on the beach, which is a ten minute walk down the road from the centre of the village itself. The beach is part of Kiotari Bay, so it's not cozy, but it is very quiet even during high season. It's mainly shingle, has a modest number of sun loungers and umbrellas plus a couple of well-looked-after changing huts and showers, connected by walkways set into the shingle to enable one to walk around without scorching the soles of one's feet during high summer.

It's very laid back and the perfect place for a chill-out holiday. The village has three or four hotels, none of them too large, plus a number of apartments to let for tourists. All in all me and the better half often say that we could have spent a very enjoyable holiday here, walking everywhere, in an essentially Greek atmosphere.

Dimitris decided to renovate what he's now called the Summer Breeze hotel on the edge of the village, not a stone's throw from the beach, and he's done a very nice job of it. He deserves to make it a success because, not only has he done a great job with the hotel, but he's a caring man who really wants to get involved in what we now call an annual event, 'Help For Health Gennadi'.

Not long after our event at Julia's house, Dimitris said he wanted to organise a bigger one in the village, in the square next to the village school in fact. He, being a Greek and running a business too, was able to sort out the legalities much better than we could, which in all probability meant calling in a few favours here and there, but in view of the cause everything was justified. His event went really well and he also set up some music and a souvlaki stand to help it go with a swing.

In the first year we raised, combining both events, a wonderful €2700, give or take a few cents.

Once again, owing to the crazy system here, which would allow the local authority to swoop down like a giant magpie and take a huge chunk of that cash as a 'tax' were we to give it to Doctor Niko directly to spend as he saw fit, we had to get him and his staff to make a list of what goods they needed as a priority and donate those goods as already purchased. Well, if I'm honest we found ways to do it that meant Niko could place the orders, but he wasn't able to put it through the surgery's books. It's lunacy, but that's the way it is.

The Centre was able to buy lots of essentials with all that money, but what

I'm really proud of was what I learned a few weeks later.

Julia called to to say that could I be at the surgery that coming Sunday morning at around 10.00am, because Doctor Nikos wanted to thank us in person for what we'd done. I went down there on a damp February morning, met Julia, Viv, Pete and Maggie in the kafeneion across the road and we all sat there sipping our *Ellinikos* and wondering quite what Doctor Nikos had in mind. There did seem to be an awful lot of activity over the road, with an inordinately large number of vehicles coming and going, but mainly coming and parking, plus some very smartly dressed folk who looked a lot like dignitaries hanging around. It all looked like something way beyond a quiet reception to say thanks to a few ex-pats and a local caring Greek.

What Nikos had planned was definitely beyond what any of us had imagined. Once we'd crossed the road and entered the building we were shocked at how packed it was. There were too, among the throng, patients coming and going, those emerging from the treatment room clutching a small white dressing in the crook of their elbows and holding one hand up close to their chests. There were lots of very smartly-dressed Greeks hanging around and talking excitedly. There was a small room set aside for refreshments, which was where our little troupe gathered, drank coffee from plastic cups and nibbled on delicious home-made cakes that some local Greek women had made for the occasion. After a while and after not having had a chance to ask Niko what it was all about (he was seemingly constantly surrounded by important-looking Greeks), I began to think that it was merely some kind of reception and that we'd all stand around for a while longer and then disperse. So I began hatching a plan to clear off out of it and slip away home. I was a small fry in all of this, or so I thought.

Julia has a friend who works at the surgery and she was able to solve one mystery. How come that, in the midst of all the hubbub of smart folk standing around waiting for something to happen, there were peasant farmers and their families apparently having blood taken – on a Sunday? Julia's friend told us that with our part of the cash that had been raised by the two events, the centre was able to run a screening programme for both high cholesterol and potential diabetes among any local residents who'd like to come in. They'd been able to purchase the syringes, sample bottles and dressings and were able to send away the samples for testing. The results would help countless locals, who may otherwise have found out too late, that they either had high cholesterol, or were heading for full-blown diabetes. These patients were locals who'd learned of the programme and were coming in for some blood to be taken.

Just as I'd finally decided that, yes, I'd slip away, Doctor Nikos called for everyone's attention and suggested that we all gather around in his office, which fortunately is at the top of a few steps and has one entire wall of frosted glass panel doors which can be slid back to make the office much larger, taking in the foyer area just outside. By the time he'd got everyone's attention, there were probably a hundred bodies all standing around, allowing Nikos a small space in front of his desk in which to evidently make some kind of speech. On one wall there had been hastily hung a huge woven banner for the local branch of the Lions Club. I remember the Lions charity organisation from years ago in my home town of Bath in the UK. I had no idea that they were functioning even here on Greek islands like Rhodes. Yet here was a Greek delegation from the International Lions Club right smack dab in the village of Gennadi, evidently showing that they too had been raising funds to help the surgery to operate successfully.

Doctor Nikos began an impassioned speech, during which on several occasions he filled up while trying to express his gratitude for all that had been done in the past twelve months by local people, the great and the good and the small and OK, like us. There was a very expensive looking electronic apparatus sitting on an office chair in front of him that was evidently a gift from the Lions. On the desk behind him there was a pile of what looked to me like black files. In fact, once Doctor Nikos had begun handing these out I saw that they were actually A4 certificates, which had been mounted and fitted behind glass in nice, modern, black wooden frames. He made a brief speech about how indebted he and his team were to each particular benefactor and then called them forward from the crowd, whereupon he lifted a certificate, handed it to the person or persons, waited for photographs to be taken and then asked them to say a few words. The certificates were a way of showing the centre's appreciation for all the sterling work done by various individuals and organisations.

By the time he'd handed out four of these and there were only two remaining on his desk, I was quite comfortable in the perception that, of course, what we 'Help For Health-ers' had done would be nowhere near enough to merit one of these certificates being handed to us.

Nikos then began talking about a recent event that had exceeded all expectations and even encouraged local Greeks to do something similar. He recounted how grateful he was for a group of ex-pat British who'd held an event to raise cash and then explained what the Centre had been able to do as a result. Almost before I could assimilate this, he was asking for *kyrio* John Manuel to step forward to receive the next certificate on behalf of 'Help For Health Gennadi'. I looked at Julia, Viv, Pete and Maggie, thrust both of my hands outward and shrugged my shoulders. Surely one of them would like to receive the certificate? Nope, they all parted like the Red Sea and a hand was applied to the small of my back to go forward, shake Doctor Niko's hand and receive the certificate.

Frankly, I've never felt so honoured by the local Greek people as I did at that moment. Nikos handed me the frame and asked me to say a couple of words which, of course, proved to be a total impossibility. I filled up, attempted to express a couple of thoughts in Greek and failed miserably. No doubt everyone present thought that I couldn't speak the language because I was transformed into a gibbering wreck. No one could have been more relieved about anything, even that blissful feeling one gets at the successful outcome from having received a suppository, than I was as I re-entered the gathered throng and sank into obscurity once more.

Later, once the 'ceremony' had concluded, we all stood around; me, my 'team' and a couple of Greek dignitaries about whom I knew absolutely nothing, and had our photos taken. As I type this now that certificate hangs above me in my little cubbyhole of an office.

This year I stepped back a bit and let Julia, Viv and Dimitri run the events. Of course I supported them and still run the Facebook page because – and not wishing to compare myself to the Lone Ranger or anything – 'my work here is done'.

Over the years that we've lived here we've heard rumours about the Gennadi Health Centre closing. It's good to know it's still there and still providing a crucial service to this part of the island. It's also gratifying to know that this is, in a very small part, due to the support of a bunch of caring ex-pats.

17. Italians

Before coming here I knew very little about the Italian occupation of large swathes of Greece prior to the Nazis arriving. I also had only a very sketchy knowledge of how Greece emerged from under the centuries-long occupation by the Turks, or Ottomans as they'd more correctly be called at the time.

I had no idea (I'm now ashamed to admit) that the Dodecanese islands were under Italian rule from as far back as 1912, even though other areas of Greece were only occupied for a couple of years from around 1940 until the Nazis arrived during the Second World War. This disparity, though, explains why so many public buildings existing here on Rhodes and in the rest of the island chain were built by the Italians. They had a few decades in which to set about it.

Rhodes has a splendid array of buildings that the Greeks are nowadays rightly proud of, but which are really a legacy from the Italian years. You can still meet older Greeks, especially women, who speak Italian, owing to Mussolini's programme of Italianisation. Back then, between the wars, girls weren't allowed to go to school, which is also why the few surviving women of that generation often can't read or write. There were by default many negatives about life under the Italians for the Greeks of the Dodecanese islands, but there were positive benefits too, which have also left their legacy here.

For instance, The 'Fascist program' made attempts to modernise the islands, eradicating malaria, constructing hospitals, aqueducts and a power plant to provide Rhodes Town with electric lighting, and established the Dodecanese Cadastre, which is still the basis for establishing who owns which parcels of land here. The Palace of the Grand Master within the Old Town was restored and rebuilt.

Having worked on excursions with tourists for almost a decade now I've been swotting up on the modern history and found it fascinating. There's a village in the hills called Eleousa, which was almost entirely built by the Italians, ostensibly to house farmers and their families, but also beside the old square there is a rather beautiful if bereft building that was reputed to have been intended as a sanatorium. Next to that is another building that was probably going to be a prison. The large church at the top of the square was meant to be a Roman Catholic edifice, but has since (of course) been turned into an Orthodox place of worship. Just a hundred metres or so up a side road from the square is the circular pond (with a fountain) that even today is home to a very rare species of fish, the Gizani, which is only found here on Rhodes and listed as a top priority endangered species by the European Union.

Walk along Mandraki Harbour in Rhodes town and virtually every building facing the harbour front is of Italian origin. Once you pass the New Market (which bears decidedly Turkish features) you come to the National bank of Greece. After that you pass the Aktaion Café (recently refurbished and re-opened), before reaching the imposing frontage of the High Law Courts of the Dodecanese. The Aktaion has an Turkish-influenced arched frontage behind which was the 'pastry shop of Rhodes Town'. It was constructed in 1925. It has been closed for about a year for refurbishment and has recently re-opened and it looks fab. It's a listed building and thus has to be preserved.

After the Law Courts you pass the Central Port Authority offices, then the main Post Office. As you reach the Town Hall square the Police HQ, the Town Hall itself and the imposing rounded front of the theatre are all buildings that the Italians left for Rhodeans and visitors to enjoy.

Rhodean aficionados will of course also know about Kallithea Springs and the so-called 'Mussolini's House', up in the forested hills near Profitis Ilias and situated just up the slope from the imposing Elafos Hotel. The mineral water spring at Kallithea has been there for millennia and the story goes that among the ancients that came here with their families to take the healing waters were some of the 'big-name' philosophers and thinkers of the times. The modern complex was built in the late 1920s and the architect commissioned to design the buildings was the well-respected Pietro Lombardi, who apparently also designed nine fountains that were installed in Rome during his lifetime.

The Elafos Hotel was designed and built at about the same time, primarily as a barracks for Italian Army officers. Nowadays it's a splendid hotel that me and the better half occasionally visit for a posh dessert and a cup of coffee. We do tend to wince when the bill comes though. It's a surreal experience when you first clap eyes on the place, because you can be forgiven for thinking that you've been spirited away to the Austrian Alps, owing to the architectural features of building. The views from up there are stunning and when the atmosphere's clear you get amazing vistas of Turkey and Symi across the water.

The crumbling, formerly imposing house that's concealed in the trees just a few metres up the slope from the hotel is what's usually called 'Mussolini's House'. I find it quite beguiling to wander around the place, being careful not to approach too close to the verandas though, which are rotting away and making it increasingly likely that someone's going to fall to their death one of these days, but the sense of recent history is very strongly present within its walls. It was built in 1936 by the then Italian governor of the island, Count Cesare De Vecchi, who was deeply unpopular with the Greeks by all accounts. It seems he thought far too much of himself and used to parade around the island in a huge limo, stopping all the other traffic (such as it was back then) while he passed. He did live in the house for a while, but it was meant to be only until his beloved leader Benito himself retired, since it was intended as the fascist leader's retirement home. Of course, he got hung up and never actually made it, not even for a pre-retirement visit. No one has lived in the house since 1947, when the Dodecanese islands were finally reunited with Greece politically.

According to recent reports, the Greek government is now trying to find someone or some organisation to take it on by 50-year lease. The idea being that it would rake in some much needed cash. So far there are no indications of any takers. Frankly, sounds to me like 50 years isn't a very good deal for perhaps a tour operator or entrepreneur to want to have a go. It would costs millions to renovate and I'd hazard a guess that the government would stand a much better chance of seeing it bring in some dosh if they sell it lock, stock and crumbling chimney stacks, or at least offered a 99 year lease instead of the suggested fifty.

All in all then, there's a lot to satisfy the history buff's curiosity here on Rhodes when it comes to all things Italian.

Over the years that I've been doing excursions I've occasionally had Italian guests on my trips. A few years ago I was doing a weekly boat trip which involved setting out from St. Paul's Bay in Lindos, lazily chugging up the coast making occasional swim-stops in picturesque bays, taking lunch on board with what was at the time excellent food supplied by some really first class caterers, then chugging back to meet the coach again at St. Paul's Bay in late afternoon. I'd board the coach down in Kiotari and we'd set about stopping at a handful of hotels to pick up guests from such countries as Belgium, Germany, Britain, Poland and Italy. Now and again there'd be a few Russians and Scandinavians too. When you do excursion work you very soon start to identify national traits and characteristics.

By and large the younger German guests were amiable and educated, nearly all of them able to speak English. The older ones, though, could be grumpy if we had a language problem. I soon learned how to solve that. I'd get a younger German guest to interpret for me and ply him or her with a few free drinks while on board the boat as the day passed. Everyone was soon happy. The Scandinavians all spoke English without exception. The Polish are a mixed bag when it comes to language, but by far the majority of my Polish guests were affable, cheery and always thanked me profusely for a great day out as they left the coach at the end of the day. I hardly ever had a Polish girl on my trips who wan't gorgeous too. Only saying. Merely an observation you understand.

The Dutch and Belgians were generally OK, but usually slightly reserved. The Brits these days (no matter what age group) are liberally sprinkled with tattoos, still tend to drink more beer than any of the others and the Russians are still slightly wary. I think it's because they're still not too sure how others are going to react to them. By and large I believe that you get back what you give. If I have ever had a Russian guest who was perhaps a little stiff, not relaxed, then I'd make it a point to draw them into conversation. I've been bear-hugged by Russian male guests out of gratitude at the end of a successful day out, even when our communication all day had been mainly by the use of hand gestures.

The Italians are something else. There was one hotel where I'd invariably have my whole contingent of Italian guests waiting for us as we pulled up in the coach of a morning, probably numbering about 15 or so people. Every country has its dress code. The Dutch can often be mistaken for Brits when it comes to their dress sense, which is usually pretty appalling. The Germans always give themselves away by the style of moustache and shape of their spectacle frames. And that's just the women (only joking, don't write in).

Italians know how to dress. If you see an Italian you know right away. Firstly they're all petite. I hardly ever had an Italian (including the men) taller than about five seven. But their dress sense is impeccable. Whatever they wear they know how to wear it with panache. There's always a lot of navy blue and white amongst a group of Italians. Maybe a little accent of red (perhaps piping) to set it all off. They're always smart though.

What really used to crack me up was the way I had to shepherd them to get them all ready to board the coach. We'd pull up at the hotel gate and there'd be probably three couples waiting there patiently. Glancing at my list I'd see though that I needed to pick up another four. I'd leap off the bus and check the names of those couples already waiting for me against my list. When I'd suggest that they may like to climb aboard while I go into reception to see where the rest were, someone would usually say about one of the other names,

"Oh, they're with us, I'll go find them!" - which would lead to both myself and at least one of my guests trotting from the gate to the Reception area to see if anyone was hanging around inside. I'd get to the desk inside, only to see through the glass doors another family nipping past outside and, as I was asking the receptionist if I could perhaps call a room and see if the guests were in fact coming, or perhaps didn't realise the time, the other one (or two) guests that had originally been waiting at the gate for me but had now returned to Reception too would disappear into the lift or up some stairs I'd presume in the search for the late arrivals.

I'd try calling a room and get no answer, thus assuming that the guests in question were hopefully on their way down, so then I'd whizz back outside just in time to see the family that had trotted past while I was at Reception climbing aboard the bus without my having checked them off my list. I'd hightail it out there to hail them to be sure that I could tick them off and collect their ticket when someone who'd already gone aboard would clamber down the front step of the coach for a quick cigarette while we waited. Having established the room number and collected the ticket from the family that had just reached the bus, I'd trot back to Reception to find no one around at all. I'd then call another room whilst three couples would appear as if from nowhere and breeze past me.

By the time I usually got all of my Italian guests on board the coach I'd probably run to and from the gate to Reception about half a dozen times, various members of the Italian group will have run to and fro as well, whilst others would have got on and off the bus for reasons best known to themselves. I always felt like a supervisor at a crèche whose kids were running rings around them.

I could never get mad at my Italian guests though, because they were usually always cheerful and blithe. They'd be gabbling on in that wonderful-sounding language of theirs and would eventually all end up sitting obediently aboard the coach despite my having been exhausted at their pre-excursions antics.

When we got back at the end of the day I'd always get my hand shaken vigorously and almost without exception, language difficulties or not, the Italians would be in an ebullient mood and thoroughly chilled after a great day at sea. Without exception they'd descend the coach steps with a vigorous handshake for me and a cheerful 'Chow!'

I suppose that my experiences with Italian tourists on my excursions kind of added to my perception of what the Italians had been like in general as conquerors and occupiers of these islands. Having read Captain Corelli's Mandolin and a few history books besides, I believe I've come to understand that, despite the occasional exception at Officer level and above, your run of the mill Italian occupying soldier was far happier eating pasta, singing opera and dancing the night away than he was oppressing his Greek subjects.

Today the Greeks have a number of pasta dishes that they'll swear blind are Greek through and through. The Greeks love a good pizza too. The facts tend to demonstrate though that the pasta dishes are a heritage from the Italian occupation, just as much as those magnificent buildings that line the harbour front at Mandraki.

18. State of the Nation, well, Island, well, ...er, ...Our Place.

I suppose my little personal take on life on Rhodes and in Greece as a country during this turbulent era is almost at an end. Here I sit, typing this well into our twelfth year of living on Rhodes. Where has all that time gone? There have been huge changes since we arrived, driving our 15 year-old Mitsubishi L300 long-wheelbase van off the Blue Star ferry at Rhodes Harbour on August 23rd 2005.

When we came here there were three less hotels in Kiotari than there are now and today there are a couple more huge great altars to the religion of all-inclusive tourism currently under construction. Petrol (gas, guys) for the car was around 69 cents per litre, when it was almost a £1 in the UK and the exchange rate was about 1.45 Euros to the Pound. Now the exchange rate (which has seen some huge fluctuations along the way anyway) is more like one Pound to 1.15 Euros, ugh. Plus petrol at the forecourt is hovering around the €1.70 mark ...again. Britain was well and truly in the European Union, not teetering at the brink of triggering 'article 50' which in theory begins the long painful road of exiting that organisation. UK citizens were moving out here in their droves, snapping up cheap properties or having new ones built for a fraction of what they'd have paid for such a house in the UK. Mind you, most of them hadn't a clue as to what nightmares they'd be facing once they started sending money to some of the 'builders' that were cashing in on the boom (see chapter 7).

Greece was still fresh from hosting the Olympic Games and riding high on a feeling that the games had been largely hailed as a success. No one (no layman anyway) could have dreamed back then just how dire were the nation's finances. Hot on the heels of the world financial 'crash' of 2008 came indications that Greece's finances were, shall we say, in need of some first aid – nay resuscitation, and not long afterwards the full state of this country's woes became apparent.

Politicians' careers were ruined, pensioners saw their income slashed and VAT began to be hiked to astronomical heights. News media in northern Europe painted grossly distorted pictures of the situation on the ground here and thus contributed to the problem by causing would-be tourists to stay away out of irrational fears of being mugged, not being able to us an ATM or risking starvation owing to there being no food in the hotels. All poppycock.

Funnily enough, just the other evening I watched the UK TV news on-line and they were showing a report of people sleeping rough in a major UK city. Lots of these unfortunates were in a zombie-like state owing to some nasty, dangerous drug or other that is freely available on the streets of most UK cities. But that's OK, it's Britain. Cut to a few years ago and TV journalists were hunting the streets of Athens to find ways to show just how dire life had become in Greece and, of course, they found people sleeping rough. Well, what do you know? Tell me something really newsworthy, right? Is there a city anywhere in this world where you can't find homeless people sleeping in shop doorways? Yet the TV media in the UK was really driving home this mantra that Greece was not a place to be any more, oh no.

Well, may I thank you for having read my 'treatise' on life in modern Greece, which is one way that I suppose this book could be described. By the time you're reading this you'll already have read chapter 13 (I'm so quick sometimes that I amaze myself), in which I talked about modern Athens, so there's no need to go back over that now. You get the picture I'm sure.

The population of Greece when we arrived was somewhere near 11.5 million. Today, as I write this it's reduced to 10.7 and shrinking. Following the second world war and the civil war that followed, there was a mass exodus of Greeks to all parts of the world in the search for not simply a better life, but rather a normal one. The Greeks here call it the *diaspora* and it's happening again. This time it's happening because many younger people just don't see for the present the possibility of a meaningful career here. People growing up, especially on these islands, only see the prospect of a life spent waiting at tables, or cleaning tourist accommodation and that for a paltry wage. Just as in the UK, agriculture is sadly unappealing to the majority of young folk, who grow up these days wanting smart phones, smart TVs, nice cars and designer clothes. The idea of bending double over a field of vegetables isn't their idea of a fulfilling life. It's so sad yet who can blame them? We're all victims of the environment we grow up in after all. We're all shaped by what goes on around us. There have been some stories in the last year or two on the Greek TV news or in some documentaries that have featured young families moving back to the land from the cities and starting to farm for a living.

A growth industry here seems to be aloe vera plants. Sounds encouraging, but it's a drop in the ocean really. We have a friend who lives in a village near us who's planted hundreds of them. He tells us that he has to wait three years, though, before he can begin harvesting and until then he works as a night-man on a hotel reception desk, midnight until 8.00am every day of the week from May through the end of October. He has a family.

I first began writing before I left the UK. I'd written probably about half of my first *'Ramblings From Rhodes'* book, *'Feta Compli!'* when we moved out here and finally finished it after we'd been here a year or two. As an independent author I don't have a publicity machine to promote my work, so I began the blog somewhere around 2009 and it's grown ever since. I now have eight books to my name before this one, four non-fiction and four novels. Gradually I seem to have acquired a bit of an audience, for which I'm truly grateful. I'm under no illusions that I'll ever become a household name, but no one writes without the hope that there will be someone out there who will read what he or she has written and like it. My readership is of course primarily Greco-philes and that's OK, that's understandable. What has come as a bit of a shock, albeit a welcome one, is how far my work has travelled, largely thanks to the internet of course. I'll illustrate.

A couple of years ago I was working in the garden, and bear in mind that our house is a kilometre up a dirt road from the 'main' road along the Rhodean south coast, when a car pulled up at the front gates and a man got out and hailed me.

"Hello!!" he called, a tall man in work dungarees, evidently a Greek, yet even by his 'hello' I could tell that his English was good. I waved, put down my garden fork and walked over. Now and then people passing will ask whether they can reach the village of Asklipio on this track and such like, so I assumed that he'd be wanting some information like that. 'Perhaps he worked for the electricity company and needed to inspect something', I was thinking.

"Hi!" I replied, *"Boro na sas boithiso?"* I often reply in Greek to assure Greeks that I can communicate in their language if they'd prefer. Greeks always try to speak with UK ex-pats in English because they assume, rightly as it happens, that we won't be able to speak Greek. I usually elicit a favourable response when this happens. This guy, though, carried on in very good

Australian English,

"You wouldn't be John Manuel by any chance, would you?"

Now at this point I wondered, 'OK, so someone who knows me has told him where I live and for whatever reason, he's turned up here about some work, some favour or something.' I replied in the affirmative.

"Great, I was thinking that this was probably the right house, but you can never be sure until you're sure. If you know what I mean."

"Yes, quite. I do. How can I help you?" My curiosity was running amok.

"Well, my aunty lives in Melbourne and when I moved back here to live she told me that I had to see if I could find you. She loves your books and follows your blog religiously."

I'm sure you can imagine how shocked I was at this. Shocked, yet excited. Someone on the other side of the planet had discovered my work and was actually enjoying it. How brill was that? I invited him into the garden immediately.

He accepted my offer of a frappé and we sat on the terrace to talk. He was of Greek stock, in fact his family came from Asklipio, the nearest village to us, yet he'd been born in Australia. For some reason though, after a few visits back here to Rhodes, he made the decision to move here permanently. He was skilled at something or other, I can't rightly remember what now, and his cousin (I think) had assured him that he'd have a good job here if he wanted it, hence the dungarees, which I could now see carried a logo on the breast. He was really happy and was enjoying his life in the south of Rhodes. His aunty, however, who kept in touch regularly, was excited about him having moved to the same area as me and wanted him to seek me out to see if I'd sign a book for her. He then proceeded to ask if I had one I could sell him and then got me to write a dedication in it. He was going to send it to her in the mail.

On another occasion, as I sat in the Top 3 bar in Rhodes town during one of my excursions, when I'd let my guests loose for a few hours to explore the town, my work colleague Tim told me that he had a couple of guests on his coach (he worked the same excursion, but for another company) who'd asked him if he knew John Manuel.

"Yes," he'd replied, "We're friends." As it worked out, owing to slightly different time frames, his guests never met me but he told me how he'd been flabbergasted when they'd told him that they also lived in Australia and had been reading my blog for years and had hoped that on visiting Rhodes that our paths would perhaps cross.

All this sounds suspiciously like someone blowing their own trumpet I know. But I'm only telling you this to illustrate the benefits of the internet when you're a struggling writer. I've had personal communications from the far West of Canada, even Alaska, from folk who've somehow stumbled across my books or blog on line and it produces a thrill like no other. I've signed books for French tourists and exchanged messages with Greco-philes from Germany too. I'm not saying that I'd turn it down if I were to get an offer from a major agent/publisher. I may be dull, but I'm not that dull. But to even dream of having an audience in the most far-flung corners of the planet was something I couldn't grant myself the luxury of even a short while ago.

I think that now, after well over eleven years here, I am acclimatised. I know, for example, that if I want to take the bus from the village of Gennadi into Rhodes town, that there will be ostensibly no one waiting at the bus stop in the village until the bus actually arrives. Once it pulls up and the door opens though, a crowd will appear as if from nowhere and clamber with little ceremony or respect for others' ribcages to climb aboard. It's born of living in a hot climate I suppose. In the UK, on occasions when I've waited for a bus there would be a line of people stretching from the post carrying the 'bus stop' sign, back along the bus shelter and beyond if necessary. No one speaks to anyone else, people try to avoid eye contact and then, when the bus comes, they'll file aboard in civilised fashion. Here no one wants to wait in the baking sun when it's pushing 40°C, so they'll loiter in shaded doorways and then hightail it to the bus door as soon as it's open. No one takes offence. Everyone knows the rules. Queue up, for example, in a bank and people will talk to you, owing to their naturally gregarious culture. Wait for a bus in summer and you'll be hit from all sides by a knot of people who've all been waiting for the bus like you have, only not so openly.

Go into an office here for whatever reason, perhaps to pay your water bill, discuss your finances with your accountant, have a job interview, it doesn't matter. Just about every office nationwide has religious icons hanging from the walls. Some may say that it doesn't matter, but the government thinks it does. I think so too. Religion may be important to a lot of people, but ought it to encroach into the secular world where each individual has a right to their own beliefs and conscience? Of course, the manifesto of a political party may be one thing. How much of that manifesto they actually bring into being if they get elected is quite another. The current political party in government in Greece (and I know, this will date this book prematurely! Since it's just as likely to have changed again by the time you read this) is Syriza (which, as I mentioned in chapter 4, is actually a coalition of parties anyway) and their manifesto stated that one of their pledges was to remove icons from the secular workplace. They haven't done anything about this though and it's obvious why.

Democracy isn't about the party that the public wants getting to run a country, it's more often about whichever party is already in power cultivating various elements of society to try and ensure another election victory. The current government is composed of people who, sensibly in my view, would like to completely separate religion from politics, yet to implement the measures that would be needed would be to alienate too much of the electorate and thus they leave such potential legislation on the back burner. 'Try and get re-elected' is the most important mantra in politics. Thus, if it irks you to be having a conversation about your phone bill over the desk in an office that's in every other way typical of the 21st century, yet hanging right above your head is a moribund image of some saint, or Mary or Jesus wearing a pagan halo and looking very bored (wouldn't you be?) then don't move out here to Greece. Unless you want to be permanently irked of course. I know, wrong side of the bed and all that.

Another aspect of becoming acclimatised out here is learning that you can't leave anything open in your kitchen cupboards. Breakfast cereals, biscuits, flour, in fact anything that's organic, will all too soon become colonised, often by little creepy crawlies that are almost too small for the naked eye. If you leave a loaf of bread in a UK-style bread bin on a work surface for more than a day or two, you'll probably find yourself slinging it out, that's always assuming that you spot the little bugs that have moved into it before you slice off a chunk, smear it in butter and jam and shove it in your mouth. My wife (as you'll know if you read my blog) works part time in the summer season cleaning tourist villas. She loves it for two reasons. Firstly, she's not a 'sedentary' person. She likes to be active and, secondly, she gets to bring home all the swag that her little team shares out as they clear out the fridge and cupboards when doing a 'change-over' clean.

On more occasions than I could possibly count, though, she's brought home a half-consumed packet of bran flakes or rice crispies and, before she can transfer them into a Tupperware-type sealed container, she'll have emptied them into a large mixing bowl and studied them to see if anything's moving. It often is.

You get to work with such things. Basically, once you open a packet of anything that's going to take a while to use up, it has to be transferred to a re-sealable plastic container. Be warned.

Shopping hours, now there's something else that you need to adjust to when moving out here. The morning begins at eight or eight-thirty in town and the lunch break begins usually at two. In the UK it's been unheard of for decades for the major shops in an urban area to close at all for a midday break. Here? They all do. Well, OK, let me qualify that just a little. The food stores thankfully do stay open right through the afternoon and into the evening, much as they do in the UK, except that they still do close on Sundays. Oh, and on every one of the Greek bank holidays, which at the last count numbered twelve, not counting various other religious or political observances that also bring about closed stores all over the place. In the UK we have only eight, and on most of them the shops stay open anyway. I shudder to think about how much productivity and revenue is lost annually here owing to the sheer frequency with which there is no business being conducted at all.

In the last couple of years there have been moves made to allow some Sunday opening. The results so far are lamentable, with shops being allowed to open only on a few specific Sundays and even then to the loud disapproval of the Orthodox Church. It still looks like being much longer than it ought to be before the religious element's influence over secular life is further diminished.

Returning to the opening hours though. Yes, the stores in town close generally at around 2.00pm and then re-open for business at 5.00pm. Thus begins the 'afternoon'. The evening doesn't really start until after 9.00pm when shops close and workers can go home, freshen up an maybe chill out for a while. This accounts for why, for example, we had to go to a 10.30pm showing of a movie that we wanted to see in Rhodes town a few years ago. There aren't any cinemas outside of the town on the island. Plus, if you go out to eat regularly in Greece you'll know that the Greeks don't usually arrive at the taverna until after ten and often much later, with all the toddlers in tow too.

Once again, on the progress front, we have noticed lately that some of the newer names on the high street, primarily clothing stores with (finally) half-decent prices that the average wage earner can just about afford, are staying open beyond 2.00pm and effecting a change to the 'dynamic' of the town centre during what we foreigners would call the 'afternoon' hours. Interestingly, the term *'messimer'i'*, which literally translates as 'midday', is universally applied here to the hours from around 12.00 noon until 5.00pm.

So, here we are then. It's 2017 and my wife and I have lived on Rhodes since August 2005. Would we ever go back to the UK? Who, in all honesty can answer such a question?

There are, of course ex-pats from many countries who have married Greeks and thus will have made Greece their permanent home, come what may. There are those who have bought properties here that, in the current economic and political climate, don't look like selling for many years to come, at least not for a reasonable price. Such folk, were they to move back, would have to either simply close up their house in Greece, or maybe find some long-term tenants to rent it. If they want to become embroiled in the bureaucracy that's involved in making it ready for rental to tourists (which in all probability would have to be done through an agent) they may go down that route. There are many that we know here who simply couldn't afford to close their Greek house up and move back, most likely to a rented property in their home country.

What about us? Well, we've been eating healthily and keeping to a decent level of fitness for quite a few decades now and, with all due modesty, it's paying off. Here I am, 63 years old as I type this and I don't take any medication and I can still run up a hill for a hundred metres without suffering a heart seizure or stroke. In fact, just three years ago, when I had my hernia op done in the municipal hospital here on Rhodes (I know, I talked about this in chapters fifteen and sixteen), the surgeon showed me my chest x-rays and remarked that I had the constitution of an 18 year-old. Now I'm not taking the credit for this. That goes firmly and perpetually to my wife. She it was who, well over two decades ago now, started out on a path of educating herself in all things nutritional. She it was who began to research the effects that different kinds of food have on the human digestive system, especially meat. My wife Yvonne (Maria to her Greek friends. It's complicated, ask me about it sometime) is the most informed unqualified expert I know. She could easily appear on a TV or radio show dispensing advice and no one would ever question her level of knowledge. I bow to her superior wisdom in all matters of health and diet and I don't hesitate to state that my current state of wellbeing is 100% down to her.

Why am I rattling on about all this? Well, I suppose it's my attempt to answer the question about whether we'd ever move back to the UK. There are several extremely relevant factors that bear on how one could answer that question. For instance, if one has a fairly chronic health issue that requires a pretty frequent visit to either a GP or specialist, perhaps a hospital, then one may well be best advised to go back. Not because the system here is necessarily so bad, but because of logistics if they live, as we do, a hour's drive from the town.

Another reason (which I've discussed before) why some ex-pats find themselves going back is that they didn't really realise when they came here how much they'd miss their families, especially if they have grandchildren. Living a few thousand miles away and not seeing those toddlers growing up, with all the landmark events of childhood, from teething to first steps, first days at school and the school play, first days in new uniforms and landmark moments like swimming certificates, riding the first bike, school prize days, the list goes on and grandparents don't usually want to miss all this.

Interestingly, it's the women more than the men who usually want to go back. With a few exceptions, most of the men want to stay here.

In our case, well, at least for the time being, with our health being good and our financial situation just about holding out, we have no plans to change anything. 'Never say never' is always a good maxim though. My wife is half-Greek, we feel comfortably at home in this country, yet should the situation ever change to the extent that we'd be best advised to go somewhere else, we'd not be averse to suggestions.

We don't own much in a material way. We have a bit of furniture, a few electronic devices (don't we all these days?) and a car. The sense of freedom that this instills inside once you get over this over-exaggerated stress that so many seem to put on material possessions, is wonderfully liberating. Life is about what you experience, not what you can place on a windowsill or shelf and look at. We chose many years ago not to become parents. That's not to say that we didn't like children (well, you get fed up with chicken), but it was simply a lifestyle choice we made and we've never really regretted it. This has allowed us to make life-decisions that parents, of course, can't make. You win some – you lose some, of course. I'm the last one to decry the great joys that parents derive from having offspring, but I'll tell you one thing, it's entirely untrue to assert that you have to have children to become complete. You have to have children in order to live on through them. Come off it. When someone dies they may well have left their genes in their children, but live on through them? I think I'll just move on.

If Greece and Turkey were to go to war and the Dodecanese islands became the front line, with minimal fuss we could leave and go live in any one of fifty countries around the world and all because we don't have deep material roots. I can recommend it.

The lifestyle here is very appealing to us. We eat real food and we live active lives. Here one can take pleasure in the small things, a deer on the lane outside of your front gate, a brief chat with an old *agrotis* who's passing you on the lane in his battered pick-up truck, a coffee in the village café/bar whilst watching the fish-man sell his fresh catch off the back of his truck while a collection of local feral cats hangs hopefully around his feet, taking a twenty-minute walk down to a quiet stretch of beach in high summer for an early evening swim, slicing open a fresh water melon while your wife mixes a gin and tonic to take out to the table under the umbrella in the garden, where one can sit and gaze down a kilometre of green valley to a shimmering turquoise sea, on which perhaps a couple of yachts or colourful fishing caiques are bobbing gently, I could go on and on.

There is something deeply satisfying about picking a lemon from the tree to cut up and prepare a couple of slices for your early evening drink. Eating oranges that we've picked with our own hands in the winter time is great, but their flavour, owing to their not having been transported half-way around the world is even more amazing. I love passing a few moments chatting over the garden wall with the bee men, those locals who keep hives and drive up our lane almost on a daily basis in their truck, sometimes laden down with piles of hives as they re-locate them according to the season, to give the bees a helping hand when it comes to whatever flowers are blooming at the time. I'm not saying that I have an ulterior motive, but if I hail them as they pass, sometimes maybe with their weird white anti-sting suits still in place, even down to the netted wide-brimmed white hats that they wear, they'll so often reach back into the cab after having got out to chat, and toss me a jar of their freshly harvested golden nectar as a gift. We, my wife and I, have often discussed their generosity in this regard and have decided that perhaps it's their way of showing appreciation for the fact that we've created a garden that gives their bees a ready-made nectar source, since we often study the worker bees and delight in their droning noise as they flit about the garden going from bloom to bloom. There's one particular tree that we planted as a tiny seedling, which is now twenty feet tall and still growing vigorously, that sports yellow pom-pom shaped blooms for a few weeks each year that the bees go absolutely mad for. I can sit beneath it and the sound from the bees resembles a Formula One grand prix.

That tree, however, isn't the jacaranda.

No, the jacaranda is in the orchard and was planted about a year after we'd moved over here. It was one of the very first plants to go in when what was to become the garden was still basically a builders' yard. For many years that jacaranda survived, sometimes looking a bit worse for wear, yet always producing its wispy foliage abundantly again in the early summer. It's one of the few deciduous trees you'll find out here and, of course, it's not native to this area. It's generally native to Central and South America and all places tropical. In the past few decades, however, it has cropped up more and more often here in Greece and nowadays could probably be called naturalised, although it doesn't like to be too exposed during a cold winter spell.

The jacaranda in the orchard for many years, although surviving, has resolutely refused to flower and, if you know anything about jacaranda trees, you'll know that their blossoms are exquisite. They are a unique shade of blue and a pure glory to behold if you see one in full bloom. Of course, every year when the one in our orchard has failed to flower, we've gone sailing past others on the island that have been teasing us with their effusive displays. After five or six years of this I started scouring the internet for answers. What did we need to do in order to get the jacaranda to produce flowers? Of course, John and Wendy, our landlords, are only here for a few weeks at a time and I was so hoping to discover the secret so that we could surprise them one day. I wanted them to turn up for a holiday and be able to point them at the orchard and say, look! At the very least I wanted to be able to take a few photos and send them to Wendy if they weren't going to be here at the right time. In actual fact, the flowering season is quite long, it can extend from early May right through until the end of June. Apparently though, something that I discovered is that they don't flower as profusely if they get too cold during the winter and ours is on an exposed hillside.

After almost a decade during which we'd almost given up, the summer before last I went out to do some work in the orchard and found myself staring at the jacaranda tree. I could hardly believe my eyes when I saw that it was covered in buds. Very soon these popped open to reveal the glorious blooms. Yes, finally we had flowers. It's flowered regularly since and I have every reason to believe that it will do so this year. I'm now typing this in April in the UK, having come over here to visit some family and friends for a few weeks. We shall be returning home to Rhodes at the end of the month, just in time to enjoy this year's flowers.

The garden today looks very mature and when people visit they are amazed, especially those who saw it when we'd not long moved in. Years ago we hardly ever saw a bird, owing to the fact that the land immediately surrounding the house was nothing but dust and detritus for a long time. Once we'd laid out the garden and begun to plant it up, it of course took some years for plants and shrubs to mature, but gradually the feathered wildlife has begun to appear. Nowadays we have an abundance of bird life around the villa that continues to amaze us with its variety. During the dry days of summer (and indeed winter) we always leave a plant pot holder outside with water in it and it's become the local hang-out for thrushes, blackbirds, a selection of warblers, black redstarts, robins, sparrows, plus a few varieties of tit. High above us we see raptors like buzzards, sparrowhawks, kestrels and golden eagles. Increasingly around us we see European bee-eaters and hoopoes. Once our young loquat tree began bearing fruit we began to get jays. These may not have the most appealing of calls, but boy are they a beautiful sight.

So, after more than eleven years of living on Rhodes, what makes it worthwhile carrying on? The climate, yes, the people, by and large, a definite yes. The crime levels? Much lower than most of the rest of Europe. The overall quality of life, if you can adjust to living simply and eating largely locally produced fruit and vegetables in season, is very acceptable.

And, more recently, as if to assure us that the garden is mature and the wildlife happy, as if to remind us of what really matters, we can so often look at a jay in the jacaranda tree and feel, well, content.

John Manuel's first novel, **The View From Kleoboulos,** was first published in 2013. It has been described as *"Thomas Hardy for the 21st Century"*.
Reviewers' comments have included:
"The several twists keep the reader enthralled to the very last word."
"An excellent first novel that kept me gripped from beginning to end."
"Excellent book, full of intrigue, couldn't put it down."

Novel No. 2, **A Brief Moment of Sunshine** fills in some of the details of one of the main characters in The View From Kleoboulos and thus can be described as a "prequel", best read after Kleoboulos.
Reviewers' comments have included:
"An excellent story that had me gripped from the start, had me reading at 3am, then reading as slowly as I could because I didn't want it to end!"
"The only crime novelists I read are John Grisham and Jeffrey Archer. ...in my opinion this moves his writing into the league of the well known names mentioned above."

Novel No. 3, **Eve of Deconstruction:**
Reviewers' comments have included:
"Totally unputdownable and engrossing, with great twists"
"This story has enough twist and turns that, every time I thought to put it down and do some actual work, I got to a 'oh, got to see what happens next' moment!"
"I was really surprised at how addictive this book was, and found that as the story progressed, every time I had to put the book down I couldn't wait to pick it up again."

Novel No. 4, **Sometimes You Just Can't Tell**:
Reviewers' comments have included:
"What the author does put across so well is the beautiful but forbidding landscape, the 'old-fashioned' culture and the feeling that we who are not Greek often do feel uncomfortable yet are drawn to the immense beauty of Greece and the 'Filoxenia' - hospitality shown to strangers. I can't begin to review the believable plot ...or the well-drawn characters, or the deep emotions created in this book without creating a 'spoiler', so buy it and read it!"
"Next time I download one of his I'll make sure I have a clear day, as once I started to read this one I couldn't stop to go to work, go to the loo or even cross the room to turn the light off. Great tension created from the start and maintained throughout."

All above novels available from Amazon in paperback or Kindle format and as an e-book direct from lulu.com

John Manuel was born in Bath, UK during the 1950's. He was educated at the City of Bath Boys' School and primarily excelled in the arts. He has always maintained a deep interest in music and writing, whilst having pursued a career as a graphic designer after having attended Gloucester College of Art and Design.

His wife's mother was born in Athens and his own love affair with the country of Greece eventually blossomed into his first published work 'Feta Compli!'. He wrote several articles for the now defunct "Greece" magazine and has also had a piece published in the in-flight magazine of EasyJet, the European budget airline.

He now lives with his wife in a quiet area toward the south of the Greek island of Rhodes and, since the death of his mother in July 2013, only occasionally visits the UK.

Both John and his wife are enthusiastic gardeners and walkers.

The 'Ramblings From Rhodes' Odyssey of lighthearted Grecian memoirs...

1. FETA COMPLI!
2. MOUSSAKA TO MY EARS
3. TZATZIKI FOR YOU TO SAY
4. A PLETHORA OF POSTS

A must for all Grecophiles, the Ramblings From Rhodes series of four travel memoirs traces the author's own story, from first meeting a half-Greek girl in the UK several decades ago, through visits with her family and holidays in her mother's country of origin to their eventually moving to Rhodes in 2005.

John Manuel writes in a witty, fast-moving style that has many readers falling about at some of the accounts in these sparklingly fresh Greek-themed books.

As the title of the series suggests, these are ramblings from all over Greece and her islands, with most chapters telling a short tale in themselves. There is a kind of chronology to the four volumes, but don't go looking too closely. Rather, these are books to be delved into much like that favourite chocolate assortment.

Read and savour each tale and be transported to the land of goats, olive oil, gods and golden sunny summer days.

What have readers said about these books?

"I recommend them to everyone who is off to Greece, and Rhodes in particular. Very funny, laugh out loud, and I am actually wanting to read them again on this year's holiday."

"Another great, feel-good book which I thoroughly enjoyed."

"I'll certainly be buying other books in the series."

"This author is a breath of fresh air. His work in uplifting and entertaining. I downloaded several of his books to read on holiday but have already read them. I'll just have to hope that he writes some more soon."

All Books available from Amazon worldwide in both paperback and Kindle format.

Follow John Manuel's ongoing Greek adventures on his blog:

http://ramblingsfromrhodes.blogspot.com/